Smart WITHDRAWN
Debt

Smart
Debt

Jason R. Rich

EP Entrepreneur®Press

Editorial Director: Jere Calmes
Cover Design: Pay Fan
Editorial and Production Services: CWL Publishing Enterprises, Inc., Madison,
Wisconsin, www.cwlpub.com

This publication is designed to provide accurate and authoritative information
in regard to the subject matter covered. It is sold with the understanding that
the publisher is not engaged in rendering legal, accounting, or other professional services. If legal advice or other expert assistance is required, the services
of a competent professional person should be sought.

—From a Declaration of Principles jointly adopted by
a Committee of the American Bar Association and
a Committee of Publishers and Associations

ISBN 1-932531-74-2
Printed in Canada

Library of Congress Cataloging-in-Publication Data
Rich, Jason.
  Smart debt : borrow wisely, live rich / by Jason R. Rich.
    p. cm.
  ISBN 1-932531-74-2 (alk. paper)
  1. Consumer credit. 2. Credit control. 3. Finance, Personal. I. Title.
  HG3755.R53 2006
332.7'43—dc22

2006026889

11 10 09 08 07 06   10 9 8 7 6 5 4 3 2 1

| Contents

Contents

Contents

|Introduction

*T*hanks to mortgages, car loans, student loans, credit cards, and a wide range of other opportunities for people to borrow money, we're living in a society where possessing a significant amount of debt has become the norm. While the title of this book is *Smart Debt*, don't be fooled into thinking that having a lot of debt is a good thing. It's not good—it's just normal and often inevitable. It would be wonderful if we could all be totally debt-free and living within our means without relying on a mortgage to pay for our home or using credit cards to cover expenses, but for most people, this simply isn't realistic—at least in the short term. Thus, this book focuses on taking an intelligent approach to having debt, managing that debt, and taking control over all of your finances.

When you take on debt, it costs you money. You typically have to pay fees, finance charges, and interest, whether you take out a loan, finance some type of purchase, or use credit. If you're going to have debt, you can save a fortune and pay off that debt faster if you follow a handful of smart-debt principles that will be outlined in this book.

Introduction

Some of these smart-debt principles are rather basic, like not taking on additional debt unless it's totally necessary. Also, when taking on debt, make sure you get the absolute best loan, financing, or credit terms possible, to keep your fees, finance charges, and interest to a minimum. The best way to do this is to shop around for the best deals and to focus on building up, managing, and protecting your credit rating and credit score.

We'll start off our exploration into smart debt and ways to use it by helping you establish some short-term and long-term financial goals. Next, in Chapter 1, we'll focus on what debt is, describe the types of debt people typically incur, and focus on the difference between "smart debt" and "bad debt." You'll also have the opportunity to assess your current financial situation using a series of worksheets.

Chapter 2 focuses on one of the most important aspects of being able to take advantage of smart debt, which is establishing a positive credit rating and credit score and then protecting it throughout your adult life. From this chapter, you'll learn all about your credit rating, what information can be found on your credit report, and the important role your credit score plays in your financial life. You'll also learn how to improve your credit rating and credit score, build it up over time, and protect it from being damaged by negative information reported by your creditors and lenders.

Chapters 3 through 7 each focus on managing specific types of debt and taking advantage of smart-debt principles that can save you money. In Chapter 3, you'll learn all about mortgages and refinancing, plus discover how to save a fortune simply by shopping around for the best home financing deal, working with a reputable mortgage broker or lender, choosing the right type of mortgage product to meet your specific needs and goals, and then ensuring that your credit score is good enough to qualify for the best mortgage rates available.

Chapter 4 explores second mortgages, home equity lines of credit, and home equity loans as ways for homeowners to tap into the equity in their homes, taking a smart-debt approach to obtaining and using this money.

Chapter 5 will help you apply smart debt principles to purchasing or leasing an automobile. Chapter 6 focuses exclusively on credit cards. As you'll discover, one of the most common reasons why people rack up huge amounts of bad debt is because they misuse and abuse their credit cards, often to live beyond their means. They then can slip into a cycle of not being able to make their monthly credit card payments and, as a result, racking up additional fees, penalties, and interest charges that increase their debt. If you learn just a few important lessons from this book, it should be how to obtain credit cards responsibly, manage your balances, and take a smart debt approach to using your cards.

In Chapter 7, you'll discover how to apply smart-debt principles to student loans, whether these are loans you obtained to pursue your own education or loans you'll be obtaining to pay for a child's education.

Because we all need to manage our personal finances and create a realistic budget for ourselves and our families, Chapter 8 focuses on managing your money by applying smart-debt principles. In addition to learning how to create and manage a budget, you'll discover how to get the best deals when it comes to using a checking and/or savings account from your bank, credit union, savings and loan, or other type of financial institution.

In Chapter 9, you'll learn how to get the help you need to address and deal with your current financial problems, while in Chapter 10, you'll learn how to increase your earning potential and income over time, so you can more easily pay off your debt and improve your overall quality of life.

Throughout this book, you'll see "Smart-Debt Strategies" highlighted. These are quick tips, strategies, or useful tidbits of information that can help you manage your money better, use credit more effectively, manage your debt more responsibly, and control your spending better.

Finally, at the end of this book you'll find a comprehensive glossary that defines many of the terms used throughout this book. Developing a basic understanding of these terms will help prepare you to better manage all aspects of your finances.

Who should read *Smart Debt*? The answer is simple: anyone who needs to discover ways to better control his or her spending and debt, as well as better handle personal finances in general. This book will appeal to people of all ages, whether you earn minimum wage and are drowning in debt or you're a multimillionaire interested in making better use of your money by learning how to use debt more efficiently.

One of the main purposes of this book is to help you control your debt and pay it off. However, since you'll probably need to take on debt during your lifetime, this book will help you save a fortune by controlling the short- and long-term costs associated with your debt. Simply applying some of the smart-debt principles outlined in this book will help you save a fortune, whether you're taking on a new mortgage, buying a car, paying for your education, or using credit cards.

Introduction

So, what exactly is "smart debt," anyway? Well, that's what you'll learn as you begin reading Chapter 1. Whether you are already in debt or you're about to get into debt as you navigate through your life, *Smart Debt* is all about making intelligent financial decisions that will save you money, eventually free you from debt, and enable you to improve your financial situation over time.

Remember: there are seldom any quick fixes or miracle cures for financial problems. This book will teach you how to resolve your financial or credit problems over time and avoid problems in the future. But, for these strategies to work, you'll need to apply them and stick with the financial plan and budget you create for yourself, either on your own or with the help of professionals such as financial planners, accountants, or credit counselors.

Just as any new business should start with a well-thought-out and detailed business plan, you need to develop a plan for your personal finances. This plan should include a thorough understanding of where you are right how, a detailed summary of your financial goals, and a plan for achieving those goals. Part of this plan should be to formulate a budget and stick to it, incorporating the smart-debt principles outlined throughout this book so your financial decisions in the future help you to achieve your goals—not get you deeper and deeper into debt.

The long-term financial goals that you set for yourself should be realistic and you should be passionate about them and truly believe in them. For example, one goal might be to buy a home in the next five years. If you establish this goal, you must then determine exactly what steps you'll need to take between now and five years from now to make this goal a reality. Once you've determined those steps, you can take them one at a time and make progress. With careful planning, dedication, and some hard work, you will achieve your goals.

Don't worry! Taking a smart-debt approach to managing your debt isn't difficult or overly time-consuming. These are principles anyone can apply to his or her financial life. In fact, once you begin learning and adopting these basic principles, you'll begin to enjoy the savings and other benefits almost immediately. You'll also continue to benefit throughout the entire time you're paying off your debt and in the future, since you'll learn to take on new debt only when it's necessary, and you'll make intelligent decisions, so you'll save money on fees, finance charges, and interest.

In a nutshell, *Smart Debt* is all about being smart about all aspects of your personal finances and your spending, especially how you accumulate and manage your debt. So, if you're interested in saving money, turn the page and let's get started!

Smart-Debt Strategy—This book is meant to offer an introduction to a variety of personal finance topics. To learn more about any specific topic, such as mortgages and refinancing, managing your credit, or buying or leasing a car, be sure to check out the books in *Entrepreneur Magazine's Personal Finance Pocket Guides* series, which are now available from bookstores everywhere. To learn more about this easy-to-read, yet highly informative book series, visit www.EntrepreneurPress.com or www.JasonRich.com.

—Jason R. Rich (www.JasonRich.com)

CHAPTER 1 | Understanding Your Current Financial Situation

A ccording to the U.S. Government, as of June 13, 2006 at 12:00pm (EST), the national debt was $8,375,034,605,000 and rising quickly. Meanwhile, well over 185 million Americas have credit cards that total over $735 billion in outstanding credit card debt. This represents more than $8,400 worth of credit card debt per household.

Beyond credit cards, millions of people have mortgages, car loans, student loans, and possess a wide range of other debts. In fact, the Federal Reserve reports that more than 40 percent of all American families currently spend more than they earn—a trend that constantly causes more debt to accumulate.

America is obsessed with consumption (as opposed to investment.) Along with debt comes interest charges and a wide range of fees, which is the cost one assumes for maintaining debt. If not managed properly, possessing too much debt can easily cause long-term financial hardship or even bankruptcy. Yet, few people know how to properly manage their debt, control their spending, and be truly responsible with the money they earn.

Unfortunately, it's almost impossible to exist in this country without having some debt. The question is, are you properly managing your debt and using your debt wisely? Or, are you literally drowning in interest charges, fees, and penalties because you've over-extended yourself financially, you've relied too much on debt for too long, you've allowed your credit score to drop dramatically, and as a result, your finances have spun out of control?

Sure, it would be great to lead a debt-free life. But, for most of us, this isn't practical or realistic. Thus, it's important that we utilize "smart debt" in order to maintain control over our finances. The concept of what "smart debt" is and how it can benefit you will be explored throughout this book. It applies to different types of debt in different ways.

In this chapter, you'll discover what debt is. You'll also learn about the many types of debt everyday people utilize and the costs associated with that debt. You'll then have the opportunity to calculate your own current debt in order to determine your overall financial situation right now. Chances are, if you have debt right now, there are ways to better manage it. This is something you'll learn to do by reading this book.

If you'll be acquiring debt in the future, such as a mortgage, a car loan, utilizing credit cards, or applying for student loans, for example, there are strategies you can implement to save money and better control your long-term finances. As you'll soon discover, each chapter of this book focuses on managing and effectively utilizing a different type of debt.

Meanwhile, if you've already managed to get yourself into financial trouble by acquiring too much debt, this book will help you remedy the situation over time. It's important to understand that if you're having financial problems as a result of excessive debt, you're definitely not alone. As of 2006, the average college graduate begins his or her post-college experience with at least $10,000 in credit card debt. This is in addition to owing student loans and possibly possessing a car loan, for example. Yet, few colleges teach people how to properly manage their debt. The trick is to take control over your debt, transform it into "smart debt," and pay off that debt in a timely manner—before the situation gets so far out of control that your credit score nosedives and you need to contemplate bankruptcy.

What Is Debt?

Debt is simply borrowed money. Whether the amount borrowed is secured or unsecured, or for a long term or a short term, when you borrow money for whatever reason from a creditor, a lender, or even your best friends, you're acquiring debt. As you'll discover in the next section, there are many types of debt.

Acquiring debt potentially allows you to spend more money than you currently have in order to purchase something you couldn't otherwise afford. In some cases, you can actually use debt to your advantage in order to leverage the money you already have—but we'll get into that later.

When you acquire debt, you must ultimately pay off that debt—often with interest, finance charges, and fees. The amount of interest you pay and how long you have to pay the debt are determined by the terms of the loan or credit. The interest rate for the loan or credit can be *fixed* (meaning it doesn't change for the life of the debt) or it can be *variable* (meaning it changes based on changes with the prime rate, for example). The interest you pay and the charges and fees imposed by the creditor or lender are the cost of using the money. This concept will also be explained in greater detail shortly.

Here are five other terms you'll need to understand as we proceed:

- **Credit**—This is financial trust, fundamentally expressed in terms of an amount of money that a lender or a creditor is willing to allow as debt. Using credit costs money—interest and fees.
- **Interest rate**—A charge for using money from a lender or a creditor, generally expressed as a percentage of the amount of the debt.
- **APR** (annual percentage rate)—This is the yearly cost of using money, including all fees and costs for acquiring a loan or using credit, expressed as a percentage. All lenders and creditors are obligated by law to disclose the APR.
- **Credit rating**—This is an educated estimate of a person's creditworthiness, a prediction of the likelihood that the person will pay a debt and the extent to which the lender is protected in the event of default.
- **Credit score**—This is a mathematical calculation of a person's creditworthiness, in which a credit-reporting agency applies a complex formula to his or her current financial situation and credit history and generates a number between 300 and 850.

In Chapter 2, you'll discover how your credit history, credit rating, and credit score directly determine how much you'll pay in interest and fees to use money, whether it's a credit card, a car loan, or a mortgage, to mention only three common types of debt. A person with a documented history of properly managing their finances, paying their bills on time, making timely payments on loans and outstanding debts, and using their credit appropriately will ultimately receive the best deals from creditors and lenders. This person represents the least risk to lenders and creditors and enjoys the greatest trust.

So, maintaining an above-average credit score (another topic explored in Chapter 2) enables you to receive the best credit terms, financing deals, and loan terms from most creditors and lenders—if you know how to shop around and if you fully understand how the credit or loan deals work. The most important question to ask is "By borrowing this money, will I be able to achieve my financial goals and receive the financial benefits I desire, or am I paying interest charges and fees for a loan I don't want, don't really need, and/or can't afford to pay back?"

As you manage your finances, it may be necessary or even wise to borrow money and acquire debt for a variety of reasons. If you are able to manage your debt properly, keep it under control, and ensure that the costs don't get out of control, that's "smart debt."

Types of Debt

Throughout this book, you'll learn about a wide range of loans, credit and financing opportunities, and other ways to borrow money and acquire debt. You'll also discover how to save money and manage your finances properly as you take on debts and find out about some of the most common pitfalls to avoid as you manage your finances and debt.

The many types of credit and loans (debt) include the following:

- auto loans
- business loans
- credit cards
- mortgages
- other types of unsecured loans, including "payday lending" and borrowing from friends and relatives
- checking account overdraft protection
- second mortgages, home equity loans, and home equity lines of credit
- student loans

"Smart Debt" vs. Bad Debt

Fifty years ago, debt was considered shameful. With the exception of traditional, fixed-rate 20- or 30-year mortgages and perhaps car loans, people paid for items only when they could afford them, using their savings. If people wanted to buy things for which they could not pay cash, they could often use layaway: they would make a deposit on merchandise and then make payments, taking possession of the merchandise only after they had paid in full.

Now our society is "buy now, pay later." People rely on credit, loans, and financing to pay for almost everything—including their everyday living expenses. As you'll discover, this doesn't usually make financial sense.

When you picked up this book and saw the title, *Smart Debt*, what were you thinking? Don't confuse *smart debt* with *good debt*. Obviously, nobody wants to have debt. However, because debt has become commonplace for so many people, this book uses the term "smart debt" for debt that meets the following requirements.

Smart debt is:

- Debt that has the lowest possible rates and fees associated with it
- Debt that was acquired based on absolute need, not frivolous purchases or irresponsible spending
- Debt that allows you to improve your quality of life, not simply cover your everyday living expenses or pay for past expenditures
- Debt that comes with a plan (that you create in advance) for paying it off in the shortest term possible

Taking out a mortgage to purchase a home is an example of smart debt, assuming you've taken the time to shop around for the best deal possible, and you're paying the lowest interest rate and fees for which you qualify. A mortgage is an example of smart debt because buying a home allows you to improve your quality of life, own an asset that you expect to increase in value, and build up your net worth over time as you gain equity in the home.

OK, it's time for a pop quiz. Now that you know what *smart debt* is, can you figure out what *bad debt* is and determine if you're guilty of acquiring bad debt?

If you have bad debt, you're certainly not alone. Credit card companies, banks, creditors, lenders, and other financial institutions generate tremendous profits as a result of consumers racking up bad debt. Throughout this book, you'll see many examples of bad debt and learn how to avoid it.

SMART DEBT

Let's take a look at one simple example right now. Suppose you have a credit card that carries an 18-percent interest rate. Instead of using this credit card to purchase only important, big-ticket items you need but couldn't otherwise afford, you use it to cover your ongoing living expenses, such as your dry cleaning bills, groceries, clothing, and dining out. Now, instead of paying off your balance at the end of each month, you make only the minimum payment. (That's the least a credit card holder must pay to keep the account from going into default, triggering a negative report to the credit reporting agencies. The minimum is typically about 2.0 or 2.5 percent of the balance.)

As each month passes, your credit card balance rises—and so does the interest you're paying to live beyond your means.

That's an example of bad debt: paying for everyday expenses with a credit card charging a high interest rate. These are expenses you should be able to cover with your income. Suppose you charge a $100 dinner for two on your credit card. If you pay only the minimum each month on your credit card for that $100 meal, it would take you 11 months to pay it off and it would cost you $109.16. An extra $9.16 in interest charges may not sound like a lot, but that's for just one single purchase. If you use your credit card here and there— it's so convenient!—for common expenses, the monthly interest charges you pay could be in the hundreds of dollars or more.

In each chapter of this book that explores a different type of debt, you'll learn the difference between *smart debt* and *bad debt* and learn how to develop strategies to avoid bad debt altogether. You'll also discover strategies for converting bad debt into smart debt as you create and implement plans to pay off that debt completely.

As a general rule, don't use credit to purchase things with no lasting monetary value, such as meals, vacations, gas, or groceries. For items with a small monetary value, such as clothing or sports equipment, develop a plan for paying off that debt in six months or less. If you buy items that have some monetary value, such as consumer electronics, jewelry, and furniture, develop a plan to pay for these items in 12 to 24 months—if you must use credit. Before making such purchases, however, calculate how much you'll be spending in interest and determine if the purchase is still worthwhile.

For example, if you purchase a $3,000 laptop computer using a credit card with an 18-percent interest rate and then make only the minimum payments, it'll take you 263 months to pay for that computer and you'll be paying $4,115 in interest. Is the computer really worth $7,115? Won't it be obsolete before the 263 months (almost 22 years!) are over? If you could use a lower-interest credit card to buy the computer and then develop a plan to pay off the loan in 12 to 24 months, this would be an example of using a "smart debt" strategy.

Determining Your Current Financial Situation

Before we start exploring all of the types of loans and credit opportunities, let's get a clear picture of your current financial situation. This will help you to determine whether or not taking on additional debt is smart at this time. If you've already accrued a significant amount of debt, knowing exactly where you stand will help you create a methodical plan for paying it off.

To evaluate your financial situation, we'll look at several areas of your financial life:

- income
- savings and investments
- monthly living expenses
- current debt

The following worksheets will help you analyze all aspects of your current personal financial situation. Later, we'll focus on your short-term and long-term financial goals and get you started on achieving them through proper financial planning and better money management.

Begin by collecting your bank statements, pay stubs, W-2 forms, receipts, bills, credit card statements, and other financial documents. This information will help you complete the following worksheets. You will then use these worksheets to examine your current financial situation.

INCOME

This simple worksheet 1-1 on the next page will help you calculate your current income. In this case, we'll use "income" to refer to your net take-home pay *after* taxes. If you're married or have a multiple-income family, be sure to calculate your own earnings combined with your spouse's earnings. (Note: Calculate your income only as your take-home pay, after state and federal taxes are deducted).

Current Salary (including any tips, commissions, and bonuses)	$
Spouse's Salary	$
Other Sources of Income (taxable interest, alimony, child support, investment dividends, etc.)	$
Total Average Monthly Income	$

Worksheet 1-1. Income

SAVINGS AND INVESTMENTS

This worksheet will help you determine how much money you have available in cash or liquid assets and other investments. Ideally, after you pay all of your monthly living expenses and bills, you'll want to have money left over that you can save or invest. One of the first signs of financial trouble is when you must tap into your savings or investments in order to cover your everyday expenses from month to month.

Checking Account Balance(s)	$
Investments (stocks, bonds, mutual funds, etc.)	$
Retirement Fund Contribution(s)	$
Savings Account Balance(s)	$
Other Savings	$
Total Savings	$

Worksheet 1-2. Savings and investments

MONTHLY LIVING EXPENSES

Now that you know how much money you have coming in each month (your income) and how much money you have in savings and investments, let's calculate how much you spend each month on living expenses. (Note: A more detailed worksheet for listing your monthly expenses in order to create a budget is offered in Chapter 8.)

Car Expenses (monthly car payment, gas, repairs, etc.)	$
Child Support	$
Clothing Expenses	$
Entertainment	$
Food	$
Gifts	$
Insurance (health insurance, car insurance, life insurance, renter's insurance, etc.)	$
Medical Expenses	$
Rent	$
Utilities (electric, gas, phone, Internet access, cell phone, etc.)	$
Other Expenses	$
Total Monthly Expenses	$

Worksheet 1-3. Monthly Living Expenses

Your income should be greater than the total of your monthly living expenses. If not, you're living beyond your means: with each passing month, you're acquiring additional debt. To remedy this situation, you'll need to start changing your spending habits immediately. Don't rely on your savings, investments, credit cards, and other types of debts to pay your ongoing living expenses.

CURRENT DEBT

Your current debt represents how much money you owe to other people and how much you're paying each month in interest and loan- and credit-related fees. Your debt can take on many forms. Before we start learning about "smart debt" and how to eliminate all of your debt over time, it's important to understand your current debt and then evaluate that debt to determine if you can transform it into smart debt as you're paying it off.

MORTGAGES AND OTHER LOANS SECURED
BY HOME AND PROPERTY

Let's start off by looking at the debts that are largest for most people—mortgages and other loans that are secured by home and property, such as home equity lines of credit and home equity loans.

A *mortgage* is a loan for which a home is used as collateral. If the borrower fails to make the monthly payments on the mortgage, the lender could foreclose on the property.

In the past, a traditional mortgage was available from a bank, a credit union, or a savings and loan and it had a fixed interest rate for 15, 20, 25, or 30 years. This is a fixed-rate mortgage. To qualify, a borrower needed to have a high credit score, be employed, have enough money to cover a down payment of 20 percent of the property's sale price, and meet other criteria.

Today, there are hundreds of mortgage products available and the qualification requirements are dramatically different, in many cases less stringent. This makes it possible for more people than ever before to get approved for mortgages and become homeowners.

A *home equity loan* is a type of second mortgage. A lender gives the borrower a lump sum of money, which he or she then pays back over a specified length of time, at a fixed interest rate. This loan uses the borrower's home as collateral. Like a fixed-rate mortgage, the monthly payments on a home equity loan remain the same. Interest rates on a home equity loan are typically higher than for a mortgage, but lower than for other types of loans, such as credit cards or car loans.

A *home equity line of credit* (HELOC) is also a type of second mortgage. The lender commits to making a specified amount of money available to the borrower for a specified length of time. The equity in the borrower's home is used as collateral. The difference between a HELOC and a home equity loan is that with a HELOC, the borrower can borrow any amount of money, up to the specified credit limit, pay it back over time, and potentially borrow again during the term of the loan agreement. The borrower decides how much to borrow and when, up to the specified limit on the line of credit and within the specified term. Another difference is that the rates for HELOCs are adjustable, not fixed, so the amount of interest to be paid on the loan will change. A HELOC has an annual fee. Homeowners can use this type of loan as a financial safety net, only if and when necessary.

Lender	Loan Description (e.g., 15-year, fixed-rate)	Interest Rate (%)	Monthly Payment	Duration	Months/ Years Remaining
Total Monthly Payment			$		
Interest Paid This Month			$		

Worksheet 1-4. Mortgage, second mortgage, HELOC, and/or home equity loan

CAR LOANS

Now, let's take a look any debt that you've incurred to finance your wheels.

Lender	Loan Description	Interest Rate (%)	Monthly Payment	Duration	Months/ Years Remaining
Total Monthly Payment			$		
Interest Paid This Month			$		

Worksheet 1-5. Car loans

STUDENT LOANS

In this section, we'll calculate any outstanding debt for student loans.

Lender	Loan Description	Interest Rate (%)	Monthly Payment	Duration	Months/ Years Remaining
Total Monthly Payment			$		
Interest Paid This Month			$		

Worksheet 1-6. Student loans

CREDIT AND CHARGE CARD BALANCES

For many Americans, relying on credit cards has become a way of life. Unfortunately, most people don't use their credit cards responsibly and they rack up tremendous debt as a result of interest charges and the many types of fees and penalties associated with these cards.

In Chapter 6, you'll learn how to use credit cards better and not abuse them. If you shop around for the best credit card deals and then use that credit responsibly, even credit cards can be transformed into smart debt. For now, let's evaluate your credit card situation.

As you complete this worksheet, focuses on your Visa, MasterCard, American Express, Discover Card, and Diner's Club accounts. In the next worksheet, you'll summarize your debt relating to store credit cards, gas station credit cards, and other types of credit and charge cards.

Credit Card Name	Credit Limit	Interest Rate (%)	Minimum Monthly Payment	Actual Monthly Payment	Annual Fees and Other Charges	Current Balance
Total Monthly Payment			$			
Interest Paid This Month			$			

Worksheet 1-7. Credit and charge cards

Many people use the terms "credit card" and "charge card" as if there were no difference. That's not quite correct. A credit card enables you to make purchases for which the company bills you later. Most credit card accounts allow you to carry a balance from one billing cycle to the next—that's revolving credit—and they charge you interest on that balance. A charge card is a kind of credit card for which you must pay the amount charged in full when you receive the statement: you cannot carry a balance and there is no periodic or annual percentage rate.

Understanding Your Current Financial Situation

Credit Card Name	Credit Limit	Interest Rate (%)	Minimum Monthly Payment	Actual Monthly Payment	Annual Fees and Other Charges	Current Balance
Total Monthly Payment			$			
Interest Paid This Month			$			

Worksheet 1-8. Other revolving credit cards (stores, gas stations, etc.)

OTHER DEBTS

Using this worksheet, include all of your other outstanding debt, including unsecured loans, medical bills, alimony payments, and money you've borrowed from friends or relatives, etc.

Type of Debt	Creditor/ Lender	Amount Owed	Interest Rate	Monthly Payment
Total Monthly Payment				$
Interest Paid This Month				$

Worksheet 1-9. Other debts

SUMMARY OF DEBTS AND DEBT-RELATED EXPENSES

This worksheet will help you summarize all of your debt. Enter the totals from the previous worksheets and add up all of their totals here.

Type of Debt	Monthly Payment	Total Debt
Mortgage Worksheet #4 Totals	$	$
Car Loans Worksheet #5 Totals	$	$
School/Education Loans Worksheet #6 Totals	$	$
Credit Cards Worksheet #7 Totals	$	$
Other Revolving Credit Worksheet #8 Totals	$	$
Other Debts Worksheet #9 Totals	$	$
Totals	$	$

Worksheet 1-10. Summary of debts and debt-related expenses

SO, WHERE DO YOU STAND FINANCIALLY?

You will be referring back to these worksheets as you read this book. Right now, however, let's do a simple mathematical calculation to determine where you stand financially.

Are you currently living beyond your means? If so, by how much? Here's an easy way to find out.

First, add together the total monthly expenses/payments from Worksheet #3 (Monthly Living Expenses) and Worksheet #10 (Debts and Debt-Related Expenses). Second, subtract that total from the total of Worksheet #1 (Income).

If the difference is positive, this means you're able to cover all of your monthly expenses and have money left to use for savings, investments, or frivolous or discretionary purchases.

If, however, the difference is negative, this means you're spending more money than you're earning each month. You need to take steps to remedy the situation. These steps should include transforming your bad debt into smart debt and then following the strategies outlined in Chapters 8 and 9 for reducing your overall debt and fixing your financial problems.

Understanding Your Current Financial Situation

Let's now take a look at Worksheet #2. Are you using the money you have in checking, savings, and investment accounts to its utmost potential? Are your investments earning as much as they could be if they were being managed better or if you were to explore more lucrative investment opportunities? If you have money in a basic savings account, could you shop around for a bank or other financial institution that pays a higher interest rate, or would your money serve you better if you invested it in a money market account, a mutual fund, or another type of investment?

Take a look at Worksheet #3. Evaluate each item listed. Can you think of ways to reduce your monthly expenses? Chapter 8 will offer you some additional ideas and strategies.

If you have a mortgage, second mortgage, home equity loan, or HELOC, did you shop around for absolutely the best deal possible? Look at Worksheet #4 and then read Chapters 3 and 4 for help determining if you could transform current mortgage and other secured loans into better deals by refinancing, for example. If your credit score has improved since you acquired your mortgage or interest rates have dropped, you could potentially save a fortune by refinancing. Likewise, if you were to refinance using a different type of mortgage product, you could also potentially save money.

As you evaluate your debts listed in Worksheet #5, read Chapter 5 to learn strategies for saving money when financing an auto or refinancing. Whether you hold a car loan now or you plan to finance a car in the future, Chapter 5 will help you take a smart-debt approach to auto financing.

If you are paying off student loans (Worksheet #6) or if you plan to take out student loans to attend college or to help put kids through college, you'll definitely want to read Chapter 7 for strategies on how to transform student loans into smart debt.

Many Americans who possess debt have significant credit card balances on a handful of credit cards and charge cards. As you review the information from Worksheet #7 and #8, be sure to read Chapter 6 for information about properly acquiring, managing, and paying off credit card debt. The first step is to transfer your balances to credit cards with the lowest interest rate and to shop around for the best credit card deals you can get.

As you evaluate your debts listed in Worksheet #9, do you have a plan in place for paying off these debts in a timely manner? Can they be consolidated at a lower interest rate, for example?

Your Financial Goals

One of the components to using smart debt is to plan your financial life as well as possible. When you have short-term and long-term financial goals, you can determine when you will need large sums of money for major purchases and then plan accordingly. (Emergencies may arise, of course, but you can prepare for them financially by building up an emergency savings fund over time and acquiring insurance to protect yourself and your assets.)

You may know, for example, that in the next three to five years you plan to buy a home and will need a mortgage. Also, in the next six months to one year, perhaps you'll need to finance the purchase of a car. Maybe sometime in the next two years you'll need to invest in a home computer or a washing machine and a dryer. If you have young children, you also know how many years it will be until they graduate and may need money for college.

Take a few minutes to think about what your financial needs will be. Then, as you read this book, consider how you'll start addressing those needs now—by building up your savings, improving your credit score, increasing your income, and/or making sure you'll be able to afford the monthly payments and fees associated with taking on new loans.

SHORT-TERM GOALS (THE NEXT SIX MONTHS TO ONE YEAR)

What major purchases do you plan to make in the next six months to one year? How do you plan to finance these purchases? Use a credit card? Acquire a loan? Tap into your savings?

List your short-term financial goals here.

Short-Term Goal #1: _____

Financing/Payment Method to Be Used: _____

Short-Term Goal #2:_____

Financing/Payment Method to Be Used:_____

Short-Term Goal #3:_____

Financing/Payment Method to Be Used:_____

Short-Term Goal #4:_____

Financing/Payment Method to Be Used:_____

Short-Term Goal #5:_____

Financing/Payment Method to Be Used:_____

LONG-TERM GOALS (ONE OR MORE YEARS AHEAD)

What major purchases do you plan to make in the next year, two years, five years, or ten years? How do you plan to finance these purchases? Use a credit card? Acquire some type of loan? Tap into your savings?

List your long-term financial goals here.

Long-Term Goal #1: _____

Financing/Payment Method to Be Used: _____

Long-Term Goal #2: _____

Financing/Payment Method to Be Used: _____

Long-Term Goal #3: _____

Financing/Payment Method to Be Used: _____

Long-Term Goal #4: _____

Financing/Payment Method to Be Used: _____

Long-Term Goal #5: _____

Financing/Payment Method to Be Used: _____

Now that you have a general idea of what your major purchases or financial requirements will be over the next few years, use the information in the rest of this book to ensure that, if and when you take on new debt in the future, it's smart debt and for each purchase you develop a plan in advance for paying it off in a timely manner.

The next chapter focuses on your credit history, your credit score, and the information that appears on your credit reports compiled by the three major credit bureaus (TransUnion, Equifax, and Experian). You'll discover from this chapter that taking steps to maintain a high credit score, repairing your credit (if needed), and properly managing the information that your lenders and creditors report to the credit bureaus can save you a fortune every time you obtain a loan, finance a purchase, or use almost any type of credit.

CHAPTER 2 | Your Current Credit Situation

Y ou already know that taking on debt costs money. You pay in interest charges and in a various fees, depending on the type of financing, credit, or loan. How much you ultimately pay for debt depends on several factors, including:

- The type of loan, credit, or financing you're using
- The length of time it takes you to pay off the debt
- Your willingness and ability to shop around for the best deals, rates, and terms
- Your credit history and credit score

This chapter focuses on that last factor. Whether or not a creditor, lender, bank, or other financial institution is willing to loan you money and, if so, how much, depends on several factors, including your credit history and credit score. While the people making that decision might also look at your employment situation, current earnings, and assets, they will ultimately rely on your current credit score and the information in your credit reports.

This chapter discusses credit reports and how the information in them is gathered, how you can correct inaccurate information quickly, and how you can improve the information in your credit reports over time. This chapter also focuses on your credit score and the role it plays in your ability to obtain almost any type of financing, credit, and loans. Your credit score and credit history (as depicted in your credit reports) also play a tremendous role in determining the rate of interest and the fees you'll pay for taking on debt.

Your ability to use smart debt and obtain the best interest rates possible on your loans, credit cards, and financing relies on your ability to maintain a respectable credit score. Because your credit score is so important, it's smart to do whatever you can to protect and improve your credit score.

What Is a Credit Score?

Your credit score is a three-digit number that expresses your creditworthiness. In indicates to creditors or lenders the risk they're assuming if they grant you credit or approve you for a loan. A complex mathematical algorithm is applied to information in your credit report to calculate a credit score based on a variety of criteria, each of which is weighted differently. The result is a number between 300 and 850 that represents you as a credit risk.

The lower the score, the higher the risk. A credit score in the 300s or 400s is given to someone who's considered an extremely high credit risk, a score in the mid-600s to low-700s labels a person as a good credit risk, and anyone with a credit score in the mid- to high 700s or in the 800s is an excellent credit risk. The people with the highest scores get the best deals.

Lenders and creditors give different weight to these scores. However, when they make their decisions to approve a loan or credit, here's how lenders and creditors generally perceive credit scores:

- Over 750 = Excellent
- 720 or higher = Very Good
- 660 to 720 = Acceptable (Average)
- 620 to 660 = Uncertain
- Less than 620 = High Risk

Each of the three credit-reporting agencies—Experian, Equifax, and TransUnion—maintains a credit report on every consumer and generates a credit score from its credit report. The information in each credit report is often slightly different, because not all creditors report data to all three credit bureaus. Thus, when you review your three credit reports side by side, you may notice small discrepancies, which is totally normal. Because each agency calculates your credit score from the data in its credit report, your three credits scores will also differ slightly.

When you apply for a credit card, for example, that creditor will check your credit history by reviewing your credit report from one of the credit-reporting agencies, whichever it chooses. In many cases, when you're offered credit in under five minutes, that decision was based exclusively on your credit score that came with the credit report. The quick approval or rejection was a totally automated decision.

When you apply for a more substantial loan, such as a mortgage, the mortgage broker or lender will typically access all three of your credit reports, then use the middle credit score in making its decision. If only two credit scores are available, which is not unusual, the company will rely on the lower of the two.

Because the information in your credit report constantly changes, as creditors provide new or updated data and old data (over seven years old) drops off your credit report, your credit score from each credit reporting agency also changes. That score, as mentioned earlier, is based exclusively on information in that credit report. In other words, your credit score does *not* take the following into account:

- Personal information, such as your sex, race, religion, nationality, or sexual orientation
- Your checking and savings account balances
- The value of your personal assets

Your credit score is a tool that creditors and lenders use to quickly and objectively assess you as a credit risk. Because this score is considered an extremely reliable indication of creditworthiness, it can be used to make automated decisions extremely fast. A creditor or lender can obtain your credit score in seconds and then decide to approve a loan or credit in just minutes, based only on that credit score.

Your credit score carries a lot of weight. Not only do creditors use it to make decisions, but also insurance companies use it when issuing new policies, employers can use credit scores and information from credit reports to help with hiring decisions, and landlords often use this data to help determine how responsible a potential tenant would be.

Your credit score is an important number that you need to protect. If you make irresponsible or bad financial decisions, pay your bills late, or apply for too much credit, this can work against you and dramatically lower your credit score. Remember: your credit score helps creditors and lenders decide not only whether or not to grant you credit or a loan but also what interest rate and fees to make you pay for using that credit or taking out that loan. Having a below-average credit score will cost you a lot of money now and in the future, because you will be paying much higher interest rates and fees than someone with excellent credit.

How Your Credit Score Is Calculated

As mentioned earlier, your credit score is calculated from data in your credit report using a proprietary mathematical formula that is adjusted periodically as consumer trends change. Each of the three credit-reporting agencies (credit bureaus) uses its own version of this formula, but each calculates your credit score based on the following criteria:

- **Your payment history.** This criterion takes into account your payments on credit cards, retail accounts, mortgage, auto loan, etc.—how many late payments, by how much time, and how much money as well as each current account that's listed as "paid as agreed." It also takes into account any negative information in the public records section of your credit report, such as bankruptcy, judgments, lawsuits, liens, wage attachments, collection items, etc.
- **The amounts you owe.** This criterion takes into account the amount of money you owe on accounts, the types of accounts, the number of accounts you have with balances, the portion of each credit line used, and the portion of installment loan amounts still owing.
- **The length of your credit history.** This criterion takes into account the length of time that each account has been open and the length of time since the last activity on the account.
- **New credit.** This criterion covers the number of newly opened accounts, the number of recent credit inquiries, the time that's passed since you last opened an account, and the time since the most recent inquiries about your credit history.
- **Types of credit used.** This criterion considers the number of accounts and the types—car loans, mortgages, credit cards, and so forth.

All of this information is used in calculating your credit score. However, your payment history and the amounts you owe count for about 65 percent of your score. The amount of weight each piece of information is given will vary dramatically from person to person, depending on his or her overall credit profile. However, payment history—positive or negative—is typically weighted the heaviest in calculating the credit score. Thus, late payments and other negative information will lower your score, while a positive record of timely payments will boost your score.

That's a quick look at how the credit-reporting agencies calculate your credit scores. However, no matter how each agency calculates its score for you, the three scores will carry equal weight with creditors and lenders.

Credit Score and FICO Score: What's the Difference?

Fair Isaac Corporation is the company that created credit scores, called FICO Scores, in 1958. These scores are used by all three credit reporting agencies as well as over 70 percent of all creditors and lenders. Thus, it's your FICO Score that's important. However, each of the three credit bureaus calculates that FICO Score slightly differently, although all three will range between 300 and 850. A genuine FICO Score is labeled "Officially Certified FICO Credit Score," as opposed to just "credit score," "power score," or some other term.

Each of the three credit-reporting agencies, as well as certain creditors, also calculate its own version of each consumer's credit score that's based on information in its own credit report for that consumer. These scores are simply called "credit scores," which may or may not be the actual scores that lenders and creditors use to make their decisions.

When you request a copy of your credit report and credit score, make sure the credit score you receive is your genuine FICO Score, not a different number calculated by a company other than Fair Isaac Corporation. While a different number will be close to the number that lenders and creditors may be using, your genuine FICO Score offers the most accurate representation of your creditworthiness, based on information the lenders and creditors will actually be using.

You can know your FICO Score and be able to monitor it over time through the Fair Isaac Corporation Web site (*www.myfico.com*). For example, for $7.95 per month (or $79.95 a year), you can subscribe to the Score Watch service offered at MyFICO.com. This service continuously monitors your Equifax Credit Report and FICO Score, e-mails you when it detects changes to your credit report or FICO Score, tells you how key positive and negative factors in your credit report are impacting your score, and notifies you when you may qualify for better interest rates.

To see firsthand how much you could be saving on your current and future credit, financing, and borrowing needs if you improved your credit score, check out MyFICO.com's Loan Savings Calculator, a free online tool available at *www.myfico.com/myfico/CreditCentral/LoanRates.asp.*

HOW TO GET *FREE* COPIES OF YOUR CREDIT REPORT ANNUALLY

Each of the three credit reporting agencies—Equifax, Experian, and TransUnion—produces its own credit report. Thus, it's necessary to contact each to request its report on you. Then, if you need to make corrections to a report, you contact the agency responsible for that report. You're entitled to a free copy of your credit report from each credit-reporting agency once every 12 months. However, to get the credit score that the agency calculates from that report, you'll have to pay.

There's an alternative to requesting a credit report from each credit-reporting agency: a three-in-one credit report. This is a comprehensive report that compiles data from all three agencies (including, in many cases, the credit score calculated by each bureau). To get a three-in-one report, you must pay or subscribe to a credit-monitoring service.

There are three ways to obtain a free copy of your credit report:

- by mail
- by phone
- online

When you request a free copy of your credit report, it will not include your credit score. For a small fee (under $6.00), you can request your corresponding credit score from each credit reporting agency at the same time you receive your free report. When obtaining your credit score, be sure it's a genuine *FICO Score.*

You can request a copy of your credit report by mail by completing an Annual Credit Report Request Form (available at www.ftc.gov/bcp/conline/include/requestformfinal.pdf) and sending it to the Annual Credit Report Request Service (P.O. Box 105281, Atlanta, GA 30348-5281).

You can also call (877) 322–8228 (toll-free) to have copies of your credit reports mailed to you. The call takes about five minutes.

Finally, you can do everything online in under five minutes—request and actually obtain a copy of your credit report from each of the three credit-reporting agencies. Go to the Annual Credit Report Request Service Web site (*www.annualcreditreport.com*), select your home state, and complete the brief online form.

You'll be asked to provide your full name, date of birth, Social Security number, and current address. If you've lived at your current address for less than two years, you'll also be asked for your previous address. At the bottom of the on-screen questionnaire will be a security code in a multi-colored box. At the appropriate prompt, enter this security code and click the "Next" icon.

You will now be prompted to select one or more of the credit-reporting agencies from which you want to request a credit report. Then click the "Next" icon.

At this point, you will be transferred to the Web site of each credit-reporting agency you've selected, one at a time, to obtain your free credit report. At each agency's Web site, you'll be asked a few security questions to verify your identity. After you answer the questions correctly, your credit report will be displayed. Choose the "Print Your Report" option to view a printer-friendly version of your credit report and print it out.

Then click the "Return to AnnualCreditReport.com" icon at the top of the screen. You'll then be transferred to the Web site of the next credit-reporting agency you've selected or returned to AnnualCreditReport.com.

OBTAINING CREDIT REPORTS MORE FREQUENTLY

If you want to obtain copies of your credit report more frequently than once every 12 months, there are two ways to do this. You can purchase single copies of your report from each of the credit-reporting agencies or you can subscribe to a credit monitoring service that includes unlimited access to your credit report (and potentially your credit score) for a monthly fee.

To purchase single copies of your credit report from each of the three credit reporting agencies, for about $10 each, contact the agencies directly:

- **Equifax**—(800) 685-1111 / www.equifax.com
- **Experian**—(888) 397-3742 / www.experian.com
- **TransUnion**—(800) 916-8800 / www.transunion.com

You can also purchase a copy of your credit report with a corresponding credit score. For an additional fee, you can also obtain a three-in-one credit report (as described above). Some of these three-in-one reports include credit scores. The consumer division of each of these agencies also offers online-based credit-monitoring services.

WHAT ABOUT YOUR CREDIT SCORE?

As mentioned earlier, you're entitled to a free copy of your credit report every 12 months, but the credit-reporting agencies will charge you for your credit score. At the time you request a free copy of your credit report, you may receive an offer to purchase your corresponding credit score and receive the report and score at the same time, for a charge of about $6 per score.

You can also contact each of the three credit-reporting agencies to purchase your credit score, either with your credit report or separately. It's definitely a good idea to purchase your credit score at the same time you obtain a copy of your credit report. It's virtually impossible for a consumer to review his or her credit report and calculate or even estimate the corresponding credit score. So, it's worth paying a little for this vital piece of information that will ultimately determine whether or not you're creditworthy or approved for a loan.

THREE-IN-ONE CREDIT REPORTS

Many companies, including the three major credit-reporting agencies, offer comprehensive, three-in-one credit reports that provide detailed information from all three agencies. This allows you to quickly review and compare content from all three reports at once. The price for a three-in-one report will vary, based on the company you use to retrieve it and whether or not the corresponding credit scores are included. Expect to pay between $30 and $40 for a report, plus a little extra if you want your credit scores.

If you're extremely interested in tracking your credit report and credit score on an ongoing basis, subscribing to a credit-monitoring service is a worthwhile investment. For example, TransUnion offers unlimited access to your constantly updated three-in-one credit report (with corresponding credit scores) and notification whenever a change is made to your credit report. The fee for this credit-monitoring service is $24.95 for the first month, then $14.95 per month thereafter.

Before ordering a credit report, a three-in-one credit report, or credit monitoring service from any company other than Experian, Equifax, or TransUnion, make sure the company is legitimate. To order a report or a service, you will need to provide personal information, including your name, date of birth, address, and Social Security number, which is data that could easily be used for identity theft or other fraudulent purposes.

You Have Your Credit Report—Now What?

After obtaining your reports, the next step is to review the information in them. Make sure all of the information is up-to-date and accurate. If you notice errors in any report, you should act to correct the errors as quickly as possible.

If you find an error, you have a right to initiate a *dispute* with the creditor and/or the credit-reporting agency. By law, a dispute must be investigated within 30 days. If the information is, in fact, inaccurate, it must then be corrected, resulting in a revision of your credit report and possibly a change in your credit score.

If the error involves information provided by a creditor, begin by contacting the creditor directly. The creditor's name and contact information should be listed on your credit report. If you're unable to correct the error or initiate a dispute directly with the creditor, contact the credit-reporting agency that provided the report with the error.

You can dispute errors with the agencies online, by phone, or in writing. For the quickest response, dispute errors online. Visit the Web sites and follow the appropriate links.

- **Equifax:** www.equifax.com. From the home page, click the "Online Dispute" icon at the top of the page and then follow the directions provided. You can also call (800) 685-1111 during business hours.
- **Experian:** www.experian.com. From the home page, click the "Submit A Dispute Online" icon to begin the process. You can also call (800) 493-1058 or (888) 397-3742 during business hours.
- **TransUnion:** www.transunion.com. From the home page, click the "Personal Solutions" icon and then, on the left side of the page, the "Dispute Credit Report" icon. You can also call (800) 916-8800 during business hours.

WHAT YOUR CREDITORS SAY ON YOUR CREDIT REPORT

Credit reports are divided into sections to make the reports easier to read and understand. The order and the format of these sections will vary, depending on the credit-reporting agency and how the credit report was obtained.

All credit reports for consumers begin with a "Report Summary." This includes your name, the Report Number, and the date the report was issued.

Your Current Credit Situation

You'll also find a short summary of negative and positive information in the report. If you need to contact any of the credit reporting agencies in reference to your report, you will need to provide the Report Number.

To view a sample credit report from Experian, visit *www.experian.com/ credit_report_basics/pdf/samplecreditreport1.pdf.* Each item listed on your credit report—mortgage, car loan, student loan, credit card, charge card, or other—is called a *trade line.* Each trade line on your credit report will show detailed information, including the following:

- *The Creditor's Name*—The name of the creditor or collection agency that reported the information to the credit-reporting agency.
- *The Creditor's Address*—The mailing address of the creditor.
- *The Creditor's Phone Number*—The phone number to use to contact the creditor to make a payment, make a settlement offer, initiate a dispute, or get answers to questions. If no phone number is given, contact the credit-reporting agency or call directory assistance.
- *Account Number*—Your loan number, credit card number, or other customer identification number. For security purposes, some creditors list only the first or last few digits of an account number.
- *Status/Remark*—The current status of the account: "Open/Current," "Paid As Agreed," "Collection Account," "Paid, Closed/Never Late," "Account closed at consumer's request," "Paid in settlement," "Placed for collection," "Closed," or some variation. A status of "Open/ Current" means the account is open, active, paid up-to-date, and in good standing. This is the status you want for each current listing on your reports.
- *Date Opened*—The date the account was opened.
- *Type*—The type of account: "Revolving," "Credit Card," "Collection," "Automobile," "Mortgage," or "Installment," for example. ("Revolving" typically refers to a credit card.)
- *Credit Limit/Original Amount*—The credit limit for a credit or charge card account or the original amount for a loan.
- *Reported Since*—The date on which the credit-reporting agency started receiving information about the account.
- *Terms*—Details about the loan, if applicable. For example, for a mortgage, the monthly payment and length of the mortgage will be listed. In many situations, this section may be blank or marked "NA" ("Not Applicable").

- *High Balance*—The maximum the consumer has owed. For a mortgage or car loan, for example, that's the original loan amount. For charge cards, that's the highest balance put on the card to date.
- *Date of Status*—The date on which the 'Status' section was last updated.
- *Monthly Payment*—The monthly payment for which the consumer is responsible.
- *Recent Balance*—The most recent balance owed on the account.
- *Last Reported*—The date on which the creditor last reported information about the account to the credit-reporting agency.
- *Responsibility*—Whether the account is individual or joint and who is responsible for it.
- *Recent Payment*—The amount of the last payment received.
- *Account History*—A summary of the account status month by month, typically over several years.

REVIEWING YOUR CREDIT REPORTS

Examine each trade line on your credit reports carefully. Determine if the information on each credit report is positive, negative, or inaccurate.

If the information is positive, it's because you're up-to-date and in good standing. This will be reflected in the "Status" section of each trade line, which ideally should read, "Paid As Agreed" or "Open/Current."

If any information is negative, it could be because of late or missed payments or because you somehow mismanaged your credit. In this situation, you need to identify the cause of the problem and figure out the best way to rectify it. This might mean changing your habits and paying your bills on time in the future. It might mean trying to lower your outstanding balances. If the debt is long overdue or has gone to collections, you may need to contact the creditor or lender directly and negotiate in order to achieve a favorable solution. Negative information that's accurate is difficult to remove from your credit report within a seven-year period, unless you negotiate directly with the creditor or lender.

In reviewing your credit reports and perhaps comparing the information with your current statements, you may discover some errors. If these errors are in the Personal Information section of your credit report, contact the credit reporting agency that provided the credit report containing the error. Errors in the Personal Information section do not impact your credit score, but you should still correct them. You'll learn how to do this later in the chapter.

Your Current Credit Situation

In the Potentially Negative Items section of your credit report, you'll find trade lines that contain data that is hurting your credit score. Creditors and lenders will look carefully at items in this section before making their decisions. From this information, they can easily determine the cause of the negative information and the extent of the problem.

Make sure the information in this section is accurate and up-to-date. Keep in mind that a payment you made less than 30 days earlier might not yet have registered on your credit report. Only if you discover inaccuracies should you initiate a *dispute* with the credit-reporting agency that supplied the credit report.

After the Potentially Negative Items section, carefully review the other sections of each report, including the Credit Items section, which lists all of the trade lines being reported to credit-collection agencies, and the Accounts in Good Standing section, which displays the favorable information.

As you're reviewing your credit reports, make a note on a separate sheet of paper of any trade lines that contain negative information that you need to address and make a list of inaccuracies that you need to correct.

WHAT INFORMATION CAN BE EDITED OR REMOVED FROM YOUR CREDIT REPORTS

Remember: only information that is inaccurate can be disputed and ultimately removed easily by initiating a dispute directly with the credit reporting agencies. If you want to remove negative but accurate information, you'll need to negotiate with each creditor separately.

If you have a legitimate justification for negative information on your credit report, you have the right to add a Personal Statement to each of your credit reports. This is a short comment (100 words maximum) that you can add by contacting the credit-reporting agencies. If you've had a medical emergency, illness or lost your job, this can be explained in your Personal Statement. This statement will have no impact on your credit score, but it will be read by anyone who manually reviews your credit report. Make sure you have the Personal Statement removed after the situation described in your statement has been corrected or resolved; otherwise, it could remain on your credit report indefinitely.

HOW TO CORRECT ERRORS

There are two basic ways to correct errors on your credit reports:

- Contact the creditor or lender directly via telephone or mail.

- Initiate a dispute with the credit-reporting agency responsible for the credit reports that contain the errors.

If you're trying to "fix" negative information that's reported accurately, you'll need to negotiate with your creditors directly. The credit-reporting agencies will remove only information that's proven to be false.

CONTACTING AND NEGOTIATING WITH YOUR CREDITORS

When creditors and lenders report information monthly to the credit-reporting agencies, it's purely voluntary. *Any information that a creditor adds to your credit report could be removed, theoretically, if you can convince the creditor to take this action.*

If you're dealing with a collection agency working on behalf of a creditor, that agency's job is to collect the debt. Negotiating will be more difficult, but certainly isn't impossible, especially if the account is seriously past due and you're interested in negotiating a full payoff, settlement, or payment plan.

If you're dealing with a collection agency that has purchased your debt outright from a creditor or lender, which is something that would happen after the creditor or lender has charged it off or written it off, that collection agency has full authority in regard to that debt.

Depending on your financial and credit situation, to fix negative information on your credit report without further hurting your credit score in the future, consider trying to renegotiate your payment schedule with the creditor. A creditor may be willing to lower your monthly payments, defer one or more payments, waive late fees and penalties, lower your interest rate, or somehow restructure the loan to enable you to pay it off more.

An alternative to restructuring the payment schedule is to offer a settlement to the creditor. This is a legally binding agreement that allows you to renegotiate the amount owed. In many cases, this will stop interest, late fees, and other charges from accruing as you pay off the amount due, which can often be reduced. There's a down side to negotiating a settlement and paying off less than the amount originally owed: settlements are typically listed on credit reports for seven years and affect the credit score for that entire time, even after the account is paid off and closed.

Settlements must be negotiated with the creditor. You need to negotiate how much is owed, how the repayment plan will be structured, and what the result will be for your credit report after you pay off the debt. All settlements should be put in writing by the creditor.

Your Current Credit Situation

If you set up a payment plan as part of your settlement and then fail to meet your obligations on time, the original terms of the debt could be reinstated. This would mean that interest, penalties, late fees, and legal fees could all be added to the amount due. It would also increase the chances that the creditor or collection agency will take legal action to collect the debt.

When negotiating with a creditor, your ultimate objective is to convince them to list the account as "Paid As Agreed," "Current," or "Account Closed—Paid As Agreed" with each of the credit bureaus. Anything other than that will hurt your credit score. It will help you achieve this objective if you're willing to negotiate and you demonstrate good faith to follow through on your promises.

Make sure that you negotiate with someone who has the authority to change how the creditor is reporting the account to the credit-reporting agencies, such as a supervisor. Whether or not you pay off an account that's gone to collections is irrelevant to your credit score unless the account is reported to the credit collection agencies as "Paid As Agreed" or "Account Closed—Paid As Agreed."

Listings on your credit report to avoid include "Not Paid," "Paid—Charge Off," "Settled," "Repossession," and "Paid—[X] Days Late." Any of these will hurt your credit score for up to seven years and impact your ability to obtain credit in the future, even if you ultimately pay the overdue amount in full or you pay the amount agreed to as part of a settlement.

Many creditors will agree to alter how your account is being reported to the credit-reporting agencies if you agree in the settlement to pay at least 70 percent of the amount due and you meet the obligations of the settlement with no further delays. As you're negotiating, you'll have more leverage for reducing your settlement amount if you can make one lump sum payment as opposed to setting up a plan to pay over months or years. Creditors decide whether to negotiate with a consumer on a case-by-case basis, and it depends on the ability of the consumer to negotiate. It is not normal policy to delete negative information from a consumer's credit report just because he or she pays off a debt late.

INITIATING DISPUTES WITH THE CREDIT-REPORTING AGENCIES

Thanks to computers, initiating a dispute with the credit-reporting agencies is relatively easy. Plus, if you initiate the dispute online, you can typically have the issue resolved within about 10 days, although legally the credit-reporting agencies have 30 days to investigate your dispute.

If you discover the same error on all three of your credit reports, you will need to initiate a dispute for that item separately with each of the three agencies or contact the creditor directly.

If you file a dispute, it will force the credit-reporting agency to initiate an investigation, during which it will contact the creditor or lender and ask for proof that the information being reported is accurate. If no proof is provided and the information on the credit report is erroneous, it must be corrected within 30 days.

Follow these steps for initiating a dispute online:

1. Obtain a copy of your credit report from each credit-reporting agency.
2. Make a note of the Credit Report Number at the top of each report. If a report has no Credit Report Number, you will need to obtain a new copy of your credit report directly from that credit-reporting agency or from the Annual Credit Report Request Service Web site (*www.annualcreditreport.com*). The Credit Report Number on the report you receive will remain active for 90 days.
3. Review each credit report carefully and identify errors you wish to dispute.
4. Go to the appropriate credit-reporting agency's Web site:
   - Experian—*www.experian.com/disputes/index.html*
   - Equifax—*www.equifax.com/dispute*
   - TransUnion—*annualcreditreport.transunion.com/entry/disputeonline*
5. Click on the appropriate icon to initiate an online dispute.
6. Enter your Credit Report Number and information to verify your identity, as prompted. This information may include your Social Security number, date of birth, state of residence, and/or your ZIP code.
7. Approve a Terms and Conditions statement from the credit-reporting agency.
8. When your credit report is displayed, click on any item that you believe to be inaccurate and then click the "Dispute Item" icon.
9. Choose one of the options to explain why you believe the information is incorrect. Depending on the type of listing, options will include "Payment never late," "No knowledge of account," "Account paid in full," "Account closed," "Unauthorized charges," "Belonged to ex-spouse," "Balance incorrect," "Included in bankruptcy," "Belongs to primary account holder," "Corporate account," "Balance history inaccurate," or "Other reason." You can also add your own brief explanation (up to 120 characters).

10. Provide your e-mail address so you can be contacted with the results of the investigation.

After you complete this online dispute process, an investigation will immediately begin. You will be notified of the outcome within 30 days (unusually within 10 days). If the result is not in your favor, but you have evidence or information to substantiate your claim, initiate another dispute in writing and include copies of your information and evidence or contact the creditor directly.

Your Actions Impact Your Creditworthiness

If you currently have an above-average or excellent credit score, it's important to maintain it. If you make a mortgage payment late or skip a credit card payment, that information on your credit report could cause you to be rejected for a loan or be offered a loan at a significantly higher interest rate with extra fees.

If your credit score is below average as a result of poor decisions and irresponsible financial actions in your past, it's important to immediately begin taking steps to rebuild your credit. This process can take months or even years of diligence and responsible financial planning.

This section presents ten strategies and tips for improving the information on your credit report and thus raising your credit score. Taking just one or two steps probably won't result in a fast and dramatic jump in your score. However, using most or all of these strategies over time will definitely move your score upward; you should start seeing results from your actions within six months to a year, depending on your unique situation.

You can definitely repair and rebuild your credit yourself. There are, however, legitimate credit counselors, financial planners, and accountants, for example, who can help you manage your finances better and learn to be more responsible in managing your credit.

STRATEGY #1—PAY YOUR BILLS ON TIME

This strategy may seem extremely obvious, yet late payments are the most common negative information on credit reports and can cause significant drops in credit scores. It's essential to always make at least the minimum monthly payments on time each and every month, with no exceptions.

The impact on your credit report and credit score will be considerable if you're late on mortgage payments or skip any. However, paying late on other loans or defaulting on any loans will also have a disastrous impact on your credit score that will last for as long as seven years.

The benefit of having credit cards is that you can determine how much you spend with them and then decide how much you pay back each month, as long as it's at least the minimum monthly payment. This allows you to budget your money and make intelligent decisions, based on your financial situation. Simply making the minimum payments will keep those accounts from being late; however, what you pay in fees and interest when you pay only the minimum will often be significant over time. Plus, it will take you longer to pay off the debt.

One of the worst mistakes you can make, aside from making mortgage payments late, is letting an account go to a collection agency. This happens when you neglect to pay your monthly minimums or you skip payments for several months. If this happens, whether or not you ultimately make the payments or settle the account, your credit score will be negatively impacted for up to seven years.

It's important to understand that making a payment late or skipping a payment can impact your credit report for many years. A negative piece of information placed on your credit report this month will cause your credit score to drop—and the impact of that information on your credit report and your credit score could haunt you for seven years (or even longer). A few mistakes today could keep you from buying or leasing a car, getting approved for a mortgage, or qualifying for credit cards several years down the road. Think about your future and know that your current actions will impact it.

Keeping your accounts from going into a collections status is relatively easy. If you can't afford to make the full payment due, contact the creditor and try to negotiate an alternative payment schedule. People who get into financial trouble often tend to ignore the problems until they become huge legal problems. Simply by taking a responsible approach, paying what you can, and working with your creditors, you can almost always keep your delinquent accounts out of collections, which will protect your credit and save you a fortune.

It's true that your creditors want to be paid in a timely manner. However, most also understand that people sometimes run into financial problems. You'll find that if you communicate with your creditors and demonstrate good faith by making at least minimum monthly payments, the creditors will be understanding and try to help keep you from destroying your credit.

Paying off a collection account will *not* automatically remove that negative trade line from your credit report. Your credit score will still suffer.

STRATEGY #2—KEEP YOUR CREDIT CARD BALANCES LOW

The fact that you have credit cards impacts your credit score. Likewise, your payment history on those credit card accounts also impacts your score. Another factor that's considered in the calculation of your credit score is your credit card balances. Having a balance that represents 35 percent or more of your credit limit on each card will actually hurt you, even if you make all of your payments on time and consistently pay more than the minimums due. If a card has a $1,000 credit limit, you ideally want to maintain a balance of less than $350 and make timely monthly payments above the required minimums.

Show through your credit history that you're reducing your balances and using your credit cards properly and responsibly. Depending on your personal situation, it could make sense to spread your credit card debt over three, four, or five cards and keep your balance on each of them below 35 percent of the credit limit, as opposed to maxing out one credit card. If you do this, make timely payments on each card and keep them all in good standing. Managing your credit card debt appropriately will improve your credit score.

Spreading your credit card debt among several cards might help your credit score. However, before adopting this strategy, calculate the interest you'll be paying and compare interest rates on those cards. In some cases, you may save money by consolidating your credit card balances onto one very low-interest card rather than having balances on several higher-interest cards. Do the math and then take the action that's best for you.

STRATEGY #3—DON'T CLOSE ACCOUNTS YOU'RE NO LONGER USING

One of the factors considered when calculating your credit score is the length of time you've had each credit account. You benefit from having a positive, long history with each creditor, even if the account is inactive or not used. The longer your positive history is with each creditor, the better.

Avoid closing older and unused accounts. If you have credit cards you never use, simply put the credit cards in a safe place and forget about them. You don't want to have too many open accounts, but having five or six accounts open can be beneficial, even though you use only two or three cards.

Likewise, if you have a five-year car loan, for example, with three, four, or five years of positive payment history (with no late or skipped payments), that will benefit you.

Closing an account does not remove the information from your credit report. The trade line for that account will remain on your credit reports for seven years (or longer), but it will reflect the action taken to close the account and state whether or not the account was paid in full, settled, or sent to collections.

STRATEGY #4—APPLY FOR CREDIT ONLY WHEN YOU NEED IT, THEN GET THE BEST RATES

It's very common that retailers of appliances or other big-ticket items will offer shoppers a discount and a good financing deal if they open a charge or credit card account with that retailer. Before applying for a store credit card, read the fine print. What's the interest rate? What fees are charged?

Apply for new credit only if you absolutely need it. If you have a credit card that you could use, applying for a retail store card you're going to use once or twice might not be a good idea. Applying for and obtaining multiple credit cards (including store credit cards) within a period of several months will be detrimental to your credit score. Unless you can save significantly on your purchase over time and can justify accepting a reduction in your credit score, don't apply for credit you don't actually need.

STRATEGY #5—SEPARATE YOUR ACCOUNTS AFTER A DIVORCE

During a marriage, it's common for a couple to obtain joint credit card accounts and co-sign for loans. The information on each person's credit report prior to the marriage will eventually impact his or her spouse, especially when a spouse's name is added to accounts or joint accounts are opened. Consolidating all of the accounts makes record keeping easier. However, if a couple gets divorced, this can create credit challenges.

Divorce does *not* release either or both people from their financial obligations for a joint account. As long as both names appear on the account, both parties are responsible for it.

As divorce proceedings move forward, the couple should pay off and close all joint accounts or remove one person's name from each account, so that only one person will remain responsible for it.

Even if a judge orders one person in the marriage to take full responsibility for a specific debt, such as a mortgage, a car loan, or credit card bills, as long as it remains a joint account, both parties remain financially responsible for it as far as the creditors and credit-reporting agencies are concerned. Thus, if an ex-spouse ordered to take full responsibility for a joint account pays late or skips a payment, that fact will be negatively reflected on the credit reports of the other ex-spouse as well.

After a divorce is finalized, the former spouses should close or separate all joint accounts. They can do this by calling each creditor directly. They should also follow up the request in writing and make sure that they receive confirmation of the change. Until all joint accounts are either closed or separated, they should take care to make payments on time. Even one missed or late payment will show up on credit reports for both and remain there for seven years.

It will probably become necessary for one or both parties in the marriage to re-establish his and/or her independent credit. When doing this, they should start slowly and build it up over a few years. Immediately applying for a handful of credit cards, a new car loan, and/or a new mortgage within a short time after the divorce will not improve their credit reports and credit scores. They should try to spread out new credit card accounts and new loans by at least six months each.

If a spouse dies, creditors can not automatically remove the deceased person's name from the joint account and make the debt the sole responsibility of the widow or widower. The person must contact each creditor separately. In some cases, he or she may need to reapply for the credit card or loan. The credit-reporting agencies regularly update their records using information provided by the Social Security Administration. As a result, joint accounts that include someone who is deceased will be flagged when the creditors are notified.

STRATEGY #6—CORRECT INACCURACIES IN YOUR CREDIT REPORTS AND REMOVE OLD INFORMATION

One of the fastest and easiest ways to boost your credit score is to review all three of your credit reports carefully and correct any erroneous or outdated information. If you spot incorrect information, you can initiate a dispute and potentially have it corrected or removed within ten to 30 days.

STRATEGY #7—AVOID EXCESS INQUIRIES

Every time you apply for a credit card or any type of loan, the creditor or lender will make an inquiry with one or more of the credit-reporting agencies. This inquiry information gets added to your credit report and will typically remain listed for two years. For one year, the inquiry will lower your credit score slightly. If there are multiple inquiries in a short period of time, this can dramatically reduce your credit score.

It's permissible to have multiple inquiries for the same purpose within 30 to 45 days, such as when you're shopping for a mortgage or a car loan. Those multiple inquiries will not hurt your credit score: they will be counted as one single inquiry.

STRATEGY #8—AVOID BANKRUPTCY, IF POSSIBLE

There are a lot of misconceptions about the pros and cons of filing for bankruptcy. In terms of your credit reports and credit scores, filing for bankruptcy is one of the absolute worst things you can do. If your credit score hasn't already plummeted as a result of late payments, missed payments, and defaults, when the bankruptcy is listed on your credit report, it will immediately cause a large drop in your credit score. Furthermore, that bankruptcy will plague your credit report for up to ten years.

For most people, bankruptcy does not provide an easy way out of their financial responsibilities or a quick fix for their money problems. Instead, you're setting yourself up for long-term financial difficulties, because obtaining any type of credit or loans in the future will be significantly more difficult. Many mortgage brokers and lenders and car financing companies will automatically reject applicants with a bankruptcy on their credit report.

However, if you decide to file for bankruptcy, the best thing you can do is slowly rebuild your credit by paying all of your bills on time from that point forward, with no exceptions. Rebuilding your credit after bankruptcy will most likely take years.

STRATEGY #9—AVOID CONSOLIDATING BALANCES INTO ONE CREDIT CARD

Unless you can save a fortune in interest charges by consolidating balances onto one credit card, you should avoid this strategy. One reason is that maxing out a credit card will lower your credit score, even if you make payments on time. If the interest rate calculations make sense, you're better off distributing your debt among several low-interest cards.

An alternative is to pay off the balances on high-interest credit card by using a debt consolidation loan or by refinancing your mortgage with a cash-out option.

STRATEGY #10—NEGOTIATE WITH YOUR CREDITORS

Contrary to popular belief, your creditors aren't your enemy. (At least they don't have to be.) Your creditors are in business. They must earn a profit. When you don't pay your bills, it impacts their ability to do business and impacts their bottom line. Many creditors are willing to be understanding about difficult financial situations and short-term financial problems, especially if you're upfront and openly communicate with them in a timely manner.

In other words, instead of skipping a handful of payments or defaulting on a loan, contact the creditor as soon as a problem arises and negotiate some form of resolution that's acceptable and within your financial means. Forcing a creditor to turn over your debt to a collection agency will simply cause you bigger problems in the future, since many collection agencies are relentless in recovering money. Furthermore, the negative information that's placed on your credit report will have a negative impact on your credit score for a long time.

Depending on the degree of your financial difficulties, your creditors may be willing to do one or more of the following things to assist you, assuming you make the effort and show good faith in contacting them to discuss your situation:

- Reduce your interest rate
- Reduce your monthly minimum payment
- Waive extra finance charges and late fees
- Allow you to skip one or more monthly payments and extend the length of the loan
- Close the account and allow you to make affordable payments to reduce the balance over time
- Close the account and accept a settlement for less than the amount you owe
- Allow you to refinance the loan at a lower interest rate and/or for a longer term to reduce your monthly payments

Simply ignoring a debt, closing an account (or allowing a creditor to close an account for non-payment), or moving without providing a creditor with your new address will not cause outstanding debt to disappear. In many cases, the longer you delay paying your debts, the more you'll wind up spending in interest fees, late fees, legal fees, and other types of penalties.

Applying Smart-Debt Principles

Now that you understand how much your credit history and credit score affect your ability to use smart debt, let's start looking at some of the popular loans, financing, and credit opportunities. Mortgages are the focus of the next chapter. Applying the smart-debt principles when obtaining and paying off a mortgage can save you thousands of dollars per year—tens of thousands of dollars over the life of the loan.

CHAPTER 3 | Smart Debt Principles and Mortgages

Out of all the ways you can apply the smart debt principles described in this book, you can most likely save the most money over time by applying them to your mortgage or when refinancing.

Here are five smart-debt principles you should apply to your home financing decisions:

1. Establish a credit history and a credit score that allow you to obtain a prime rate or "A paper" loan. You want your score to be at least 620; a score in the mid- to high 700s is ideal. See Chapter 2 for strategies on how to improve your credit score by cleaning up inaccuracies on your credit report and having negative information improved or removed by negotiating with your creditors and lenders.
2. Find a mortgage product with the lowest rates and fees for which you qualify, based on credit history, credit score, employment/income, etc.
3. Work with a knowledgeable, reputable, and experienced mortgage broker or lender. Negotiate for the lowest fees.
4. Acquire a mortgage for an amount you need and can afford, for a term that's reasonable. For example, if you can afford the monthly payments

for a 20-year fixed-rate mortgage, don't go with a 30-year fixed-rate mortgage: you'll be paying considerably more interest over the life of the loan.

5. Develop a detailed plan for being able to afford the monthly payments on the mortgage throughout the life of the loan.

As soon as you sit down with a mortgage broker, mortgage company, bank, credit union, savings and loan (S&L), financial institution, or other lender, one of the first things you'll discover is that you have many options in choosing the best mortgage to meet your needs. This chapter focuses on finding the best mortgage product and then applying the smart-debt principles to the loan so you benefit financially over time. Whether you're looking to purchase a new home and acquire a mortgage or to refinance your current mortgage, by applying basic smart-debt principles you will save a fortune over time!

Finding the Right Broker or Lender

Over 80 percent of home buyers in the U.S. work through a mortgage broker. As of 2005, there were over 20,000 mortgage brokerage companies in America. In three words, the trick to obtaining the best mortgage is to *shop, compare,* and *negotiate* with your lender or broker. The lender could be a local bank, credit union, mortgage company, or some other type of financial institution. As you'll discover, various organizations (such as mortgage brokers) specialize in different types of mortgage products that are suitable for different types of borrowers.

Virtually all brokers and lenders are happy to work with people with excellent credit and a steady, good-paying job. If, however, you don't fall into this category (and plenty of people don't), you may need to spend some extra time shopping around for the best broker or lender, in order to obtain an approval and receive the best possible rates and overall deal.

A *loan officer* (also called a *broker associate* or a *mortgage consultant*) is the person who works for the mortgage broker or lender and who is your primary contact person throughout the application, approval, and closing process. His or her job involves working with you to help you choose a mortgage product, complete the mortgage application, get approved by the lender, and prepare for the closing. The loan officer will often work on a commission, based on the mortgage product he or she sells.

Smart Debt Principles and Mortgages

One reason to work with a mortgage broker as opposed to a lender is that banks, credit unions, savings and loans, and many other types of financial institutions offer only their own mortgage products. As a result, their offerings and ability to negotiate rates may be limited due to these limitations and strict guidelines. Because a mortgage broker represents multiple lenders, there's a lot more flexibility in terms of what he or she offers and charges.

A typical mortgage broker will handle the following tasks:

- Assess the borrower's current circumstances and evaluate his or her credit history and employment situation (income), as appropriate.
- Help the borrower find the best mortgage product to fit his or her needs, based on current rates and offerings by lenders. This includes educating the borrower about the financing options available to him or her.
- Assist the borrower in getting preapproved for a mortgage with a lender.
- Gather all documentation (bank statements, pay stubs, W-2 forms, tax returns, etc.) on behalf of the lender.
- Work with the borrower to complete the application form(s) for the mortgage.
- Submit the application and appropriate financial documents to the lender.
- Work as the liaison between the borrower and lender throughout the application process and closing.

When you start shopping around for a mortgage, you'll quickly discover that different lenders and mortgage brokers will quote you different prices and rates for what appears to be the same type of loan. When comparing offers from lenders or brokers, make sure you know the loan amount, the loan term, and the type of loan, so you can easily compare the quoted fees and rates. Other things you'll need to determine when evaluating an offer is whether the rate is fixed or adjustable. If you're taking on an adjustable-rate mortgage and interest rates go up, so will your monthly payment. However, depending on the terms of your loan, your monthly payment might not drop, even if interest rates fall.

Be sure to determine the loan's *annual percentage rate (APR)*. The APR takes into account the interest rate and points, broker's fees, and other fees associated with the loan. *Points* are fees you may pay to the lender or broker. A point is equal to one percent of the mortgage amount. Typically, the more points you pay, the lower your interest rate will be. When lender or broker are describing a mortgage product to you, ask them to quote the points as dollar amounts, so you can easily determine what you're responsible to pay.

Fees are another component of a mortgage you need to be concerned about. Taking on a mortgage involves a wide range of fees. As you begin working with a broker or lender, ask for a summary of all fees you'll be responsible to pay. Otherwise, at the closing, you could be surprised at how much you're actually paying and realize you could have negotiated those fees down if you had learned about them sooner. Some of the fees you must pay when you apply for the mortgage. Other fees will be due at your closing or built into the loan.

Another question to ask the lender or broker early on is what size down payment will be required to get the mortgage application approved. Depending on the type of mortgage, the down payment required could be anywhere from zero to 20 percent of the purchase price. Of course, the more money you pay down, the lower the amount of your mortgage will be.

Not all fees associated with a mortgage or refinancing can be waived or reduced, but many of them can. It's these fees that often determine the profit for the lender or broker. Once you negotiate the fees, make sure that he or she does not add any additional fees, raise your interest rate, or increase the points you're required to pay. After you've reached an agreement with the lender or broker, it's in your best interest to obtain a written lock-in to ensure that what you've agreed to will be binding.

The lock-in should list the rate, the fees, and the period the lock-in will last. You may be charged a fee to lock in your rate. If rates rise before your closing, you will be protected. However, unless you negotiate this in advance, if rates fall, you could wind up paying a higher rate. Before locking in a rate, inquire about your broker/lender's *float-down policy*. What this means is that, as a courtesy to you, good lenders will automatically reduce your locked-in rate, without a fee, if rates go down by .25 percent or more within your lock-in period.

If your credit is average or below average, you may be forced to work with a higher-cost lender who will charge you extra fees and offer you a higher interest rate, because you represent more of a risk based upon your credit history. If you have unusual circumstances relating to your personal finances and credit history, it's important that your lender or mortgage broker understand your situation before recommending specific mortgage products to you.

SMART DEBT STRATEGY

One way to potentially improve your chances of getting the best rates is to review your credit report early on and take steps to correct any inaccuracies or outdated information that could be negatively impacting your credit score. If your credit report contains negative information that you know is hurting your credit score, consider paying off your creditors and/or negotiating with them to have the negative information modified or removed.

Finding a mortgage broker or lender is easy. They advertise everywhere! The trick is finding someone who is reputable, extremely knowledgeable, and willing to work with you and invest the necessary time to help you get the best deal possible based on your personal situation. To accomplish this, getting referrals from a friend, neighbor, co-worker, or relative is always a good option. Otherwise, you can find lenders and mortgage brokers online; advertising in newspapers, on radio, or on television; in the Yellow Pages; or through a referral from your real estate agent.

Before committing to work with a lender or broker, check them out with your local Chamber of Commerce and/or the Better Business Bureau (*www.bbb.org*). A lender or broker may advertise the best rates or make appealing statements in his or her ads, but those statements might not be true or what's offered might not be best suited to meet your needs. You'll often find that the brokers and lenders that advertise the most and have the catchiest radio and TV jingles also charge the highest fees, and they don't necessarily offer the personalized service you'll want and need, whether you're buying a home or looking to refinance.

There are many free online mortgage comparison shopping sites. When you use one of these services, you'll be required to enter all of your pertinent personal and financial information. Those details will then be forwarded to a handful of potential brokers or lenders who will prequalify you and compete for your business. If you choose to utilize one of these services, you can expect to be bombarded by telemarketing phone calls, e-mails, and direct mail from potential lenders and brokers soliciting your business. While this can make shopping for the best deal easier, it can also get frustrating and annoying, since some brokers and lenders will be relentless in trying to do business with you.

Here are several popular online mortgage comparison shopping sites:

- **Bankrate.com**—www.bankrate.com
- **HomeGain.com**—www.homegain.com
- **LendingTree.com**—www.lendingtree.com
- **LowerMyBills.com**—www.lowermybills.com

As you choose your lender or broker, these should be your four primary concerns:

1. The broker can get your loan processed on time and has a good working relationship with lenders. You don't want your deal to fall through because the broker misrepresented his or her ability to get the loan approved and closed within a specified time.
2. The lender or broker has competitive rates.
3. The lender or broker is willing to offer you the best possible deal you qualify for, regardless of how much he or she earns in commissions and fees from the transaction.
4. The lender or broker you choose is knowledgeable and trustworthy.

Choose the Right Mortgage Product to Meet Your Needs

In addition to applying smart-debt principles when acquiring a mortgage, it's equally important to find the mortgage product that best fits your needs. Because there are so many mortgage options now available, beyond a traditional 20- or 30-year fixed-rate mortgage, it's important to do your research and to work with a broker or lender who will properly address your needs.

These are some of the considerations that you should take into account as you choose the type of mortgage to apply for:

- Your credit score and the information on your credit reports
- Your ability to make a down payment
- The type of home you're purchasing or refinancing
- Your current financial situation and ability to make the monthly mortgage payments and afford the real estate taxes, insurance, and other expenses
- Your ability to provide proof of employment, tax returns, pay stubs, bank statements, and other financial records to the lender
- The stability of your financial situation (Do you anticipate a reduction in your income or a change in your employment situation in the near future?)

- The length of time you plan to live in the home you're interested in buying or refinancing

As you read this chapter, it's important to remember that not all borrowers (home buyers) or homeowners looking to refinance will qualify for each type of mortgage. Here are some things to consider:

- Some mortgage products are more suitable for people in specific financial or employment situations.
- Different mortgage brokers and lenders have different qualification requirements and approval guidelines for each of their mortgage products.
- Each broker or lender will offer a slightly different selection of mortgage product options, with brokers offering the largest selections of products because they typically represent a variety of lenders.

The rest of this chapter describes some of the most common mortgage options available. However, brokers and lenders may offer you additional mortgage products or variations on the common mortgage products described here. Before completing an application, make sure you understand the specific mortgage product you're applying for and that you understand all of the fees associated with it.

SMART-DEBT STRATEGY

One common problem is for borrowers to consider only the quoted monthly payment for a mortgage product and not the real estate taxes, insurance, homeowners' association dues (if applicable), and other fees that'll be due each month. When these expenses are added to the monthly payment, the borrower can no longer afford it. When a broker or lender offers you a specific mortgage product, make sure you understand early on what he or she is offering. Don't wait until the closing to have the terms and specifics of the loan described to you.

Also, carefully review the truth-in-lending, good-faith estimate, and HUD-1 statements provided by the lender or broker *before* your closing. These documents will outline all of the fees you'll be paying that are associated with the loan. Because not all fees are listed on each document, it will be necessary to review and compare information on all three documents. Your real estate attorney is an excellent resource for guidance if you need information on any of these documents explained.

For each type of mortgage product described in this chapter, you'll read a brief description of how the mortgage works and the type of borrower to whom it might appeal and some of the pros and cons. Because every home buyer or homeowner's situation is different, once you understand the basic information provided here, be sure to discuss your specific options in detail with your mortgage broker or lender.

Virtually all of these mortgage products and options apply to home buyers and homeowners looking to refinance. For people refinancing a mortgage or who have owned a home, for example, additional mortgage products and other financing options may also be available.

SMART-DEBT STRATEGY

In order to properly understand the mortgage products described in this book and what your broker or lender will offer, it's important to understand some basic mortgage-related terminology. Be sure to review the glossary provided in the back of this book.

Mortgage and Finance Calculation Software and Resources

Need help figuring out potential mortgage payments and creating an amortization table for a fixed-rate loan? Can't figure out calculations for interest-only mortgages to see if this type of loan makes sense for you? What you need is a good financial calculator! You can find a variety of free loan calculators online at popular mortgage, personal finance, and loan-related Web sites, including these six:

- A-Loan-Calculator.com—www.a-loan-calculator.com
- Bank of America—www.bankofamerica.com/loansandhomes/index.cfm
- Bankrate.com—www.bankrate.com
- Just Mortgage Calculators—www.justmortgagecalculators.com
- Mortgage101.com—www.mortgage101.com/Calculators/Index.asp
- Yahoo! Finance—finance.yahoo.com/loan/mortgage

You can also visit any consumer electronics store and pick up a handheld financial calculator, like the Texas Instruments BA II Plus Financial Calculator, or download mortgage/loan calculator software for your Palm-OS based PDA. LoanExpert Plus™ from WakefieldSoft, LLC (www.wakefieldsoft.com), for example, is a full-featured mortgage and loan calculator for Palm PDAs that easily handles loan amortization and interest-only loan calculations.

To find more online or software-based loan calculators, using any Internet search engine, such as Yahoo! or Google, use the search phrase "mortgage calculator" or "loan calculator." Using any online or software-based loan or mortgage calculator, you can calculate interest, monthly payments, how much a loan could cost you, or how much you could save over the long term.

SMART-DEBT STRATEGY

Ideally, you don't want to spend more than 35 percent of your net income on housing. This includes your mortgage payment, insurance, real estate taxes, utilities, and home maintenance. If you have allocated 35 percent of your budget to housing and then at the end of the year you have money left over from this allocation, put it in a special savings account to use for expensive repairs—such as the roof, hot water heater, or air conditioning system—or replacing a major appliance.

MEET MORTGAGE CONSULTANT MARK GIORDANI

Mark Giordani is a senior mortgage consultant with one of the largest privately owned mortgage brokerage firms and correspondent lenders in the United States. Acting as a personal "mortgage shopper," his job is to help his clients determine their mortgage needs and apply for the most suitable mortgage and then to oversee the mortgage process from prequalification to closing.

Because he works for a well-established and large mortgage brokerage and correspondent lender, he has access to dozens of lenders offering hundreds of mortgage products. Throughout the rest of this chapter, Giordani offers advice to home buyers and homeowners about specific mortgage products.

Based in Massachusetts, Giordani works with a broad range of clients from across the United States. His firm offers an abundance of streamlined documentation loans that eliminate the need for the borrower to provide asset and income documentation. These reduced-documentation loans can save the borrower a tremendous amount of time and hassle. Giordani can be reached at (888) 695-3353 or (508) 291-8000.

Common Types of Mortgages

The following is information about specific types of mortgage products that are available from mortgage brokers or lenders.

15-, 20-, AND 30-YEAR FIXED-RATE MORTGAGES

This is the most common and traditional type of mortgage. Not long ago, it was also the only type of mortgage product; prospective home buyers either qualified for it or not. Today, with so many mortgage products available from a wide range of financial institutions and lenders, this is no longer the case.

A fixed-rate mortgage has an interest rate that remains the same for the term of the mortgage. The longer the term, the lower your monthly payment, because you have more time to pay back the principal. The longer the term, however, the more interest you'll pay over the life of the loan, even though your monthly payments are lower. The higher your credit score and the more you put down (and a few other factors), the lower the interest rate.

Take a look at the following example of 15- and 30-year fixed-rate mortgages for a $200,000 loan at 7.5 percent interest.

15-Year Fixed-Rate Mortgage
(180 monthly payments, excludes taxes and insurance)
Monthly Payment: $1,854.03
Total Interest Paid over Life of Loan: $133,729.00

30-Year Fixed-Rate Mortgage
(360 monthly payments, excludes taxes and insurance)
Monthly Payment: $1,398.43
Total Interest Paid over Life of Loan: $303,425.00

As you can see, extending the term of the loan decreases the monthly payment but increases the amount of interest. A simple amortization table or calculator will show how much of the monthly payment is being applied to the principal and how much is for interest.

Take the above example of the fixed-rate, 30-year mortgage of $200,000 at 7.5 percent interest with monthly payments of $1,398.43 for the term of the loan. Using an amortization calculator, you can see that only $148.93 of the first payment would be paying off the principal, while $1,250.00 would be paying interest. Almost 30 years later, with the final payments, less than

$20 of each payment would be interest and the rest would be paying off the principal. You can find a free amortization calculator on many real estate Web sites, including realestate.yahoo.com/calculators/amortization.html.

Fixed-rate mortgages are typical available for 10-, 15-, 20-, and 30-year terms from most lenders. As always, you'll want to shop around for the best rates, terms, and options.

Words of Wisdom from Mark Giordani

A fixed-rate mortgage is a great product if someone will be living in or owning the property for a long time. A fixed-rate mortgage is an amortized loan. Every month when you make your mortgage payment, some portion of it will go toward the principal and some to the interest. Historically, this has been a very popular loan choice, but has become less popular due to the variety of mortgage products now available.

ADJUSTABLE RATE MORTGAGE (ARM)

An adjustable-rate mortgage (ARM) has an interest rate that can change during the life of the loan. If the interest rate goes down, so does the monthly payment (in most cases). If the interest rate goes up, so does the monthly payment. The benefit to this type of loan is that the initial rate could be significantly lower than the rate for a comparable fixed-rate mortgage. This makes becoming a homeowner more affordable (in terms of monthly payments) and often makes qualifying easier.

These loans, also called *variable-rate loans*, have been popular since the late 1980s. The big drawback to this type of loan is that the interest rate changes constantly and the borrower is basically gambling that it will go down, not up. However, depending on the lender, you may not benefit if rates go down, but you will be penalized if rates go up.

There are mortgage products that start off at a fixed rate for the first few years, then automatically switch to an adjustable rate. This type of loan, the *fixed/adjustable mortgage*, is good if you have an average or below-average credit score, because you can qualify for a loan at a lower interest rate than for a traditional fixed-rate mortgage. During the initial one, two, three, or five years, when the rate is fixed, you can work toward improving your credit score. Then, before the loan transforms into an adjustable-rate mortgage, you can refinance and potentially qualify for a fixed-rate mortgage at a more attractive rate, assuming interest rates don't go up considerably.

Some lenders offer *hybrid* or *convertible ARMs* that start off as adjustable-rate mortgages and then can be transferred into fixed-rate mortgages after a specified period. Again, however, the borrower is gambling that rates will stay the same or drop, not rise, during the specified period.

Because ARMs come in a variety of configurations, make sure you fully understand the mortgage product you're being offered. If the mortgage will start off as a fixed-rate mortgage and automatically transform into an ARM, you want to know exactly what the fixed-rate period will be and then how often the rate will adjust thereafter. Will the loan include preset caps on the adjustable interest rate?

Before agreeing to an adjustable-rate mortgage, consult with several lenders or mortgage brokers and determine what your monthly payments will be immediately and what they could be if rates increase. While the initial offer for this type of loan may be attractive, make sure it makes sense over the long term based on your personal financial situation.

> ## *Words of Wisdom from Mark Giordani*
>
> When a bank is committing to a fixed interest rate for 10, 15, 20, or 30 years, there's a good chance that interest rates may rise, but the bank will not be able to pass that raise along to you. If a loan carries an adjustable interest rate, lenders are usually willing to offer a lower rate than they would for a fixed-rate mortgage. Because it's an adjustable rate, the lender can later raise the interest rate after one, two, three, or five years (or sooner—be careful!), for example, based on the predetermined guidelines of that loan. An ARM can save you money if it has a fixed rate for several years and you know you don't plan to hang onto that property for that entire fixed-rate term.
>
> For example, if the ARM has a fixed rate for the first five years, but you only plan to keep the home for four years, you can qualify for a lower interest rate for those four years and save money. The risk to you is that if you wind up keeping the property beyond the five years, your interest rate could go up, which means your monthly payment will increase. This can work the other way too. To your advantage, adjustable-rate mortgages can also adjust in a downward fashion.

BALLOON MORTGAGE

A balloon mortgage has one final payment that is much higher than the regular monthly payment. The borrower receives a lower rate and makes lower monthly payments for a specific period of time, which can typically be between three and 10 years. After that period, the borrower must pay off the principal balance in one lump sum. At this point, under certain circumstances, the loan could be converted to a fixed-rate or adjustable rate loan through refinancing. This type of mortgage product is best for people who plan to sell their home, pay it off, or refinance it *before* the balloon payment comes due. It's potentially a good short-term loan option for people who qualify, because monthly payments are typically significantly lower than more traditional types of loans. Homebuyers will benefit even more if the property appreciates in value.

The drawback to this type of loan is that when the final balloon payment is due, if you plan to refinance the loan to transform it into a fixed-rate mortgage, the interest rate could potentially be much higher than when you obtained the loan.

Before getting any type of nontraditional loan, shop around for the best deal and consult with a financial planner and/or several lenders or mortgage brokers to ensure that you understand the specific terms you're being offered and that this type of loan is most suitable for your individual needs, based on your financial and credit circumstances. There are so many other products on the market that it is best to stay away from balloon loans, unless there is no other option and you fully undersand the extent of the risks involved.

Words of Wisdom from Mark Giordani

Balloon loans tend to have a lot of stigma attached to them. If you don't have the money for that final large payment, the lender could foreclose on the property. Generally speaking, if you can qualify for a non-balloon loan, I would pursue that option instead. Discuss your options with your mortgage broker or personal financial advisor.

BIWEEKLY MORTGAGE (AKA TWO-STEP MORTGAGE)

A biweekly mortgage works just like a traditional fixed-rate mortgage, except that, instead of making regular monthly payments, the borrower makes lower payments biweekly (every two weeks). Paying biweekly means 26 payments a year—the equivalent of 13 months. The benefit is that you would pay off the loan significantly faster than a standard fixed-rate loan and pay much less interest over the life of the loan. You would also be building up equity in your home much faster and could cut the time it takes to pay it off by up to eight years.

Often, the lender deducts the biweekly payments automatically from the borrower's checking account. The main drawback to this type of loan is that you must be able to afford to make the payments every two weeks. Your ability to do this will most likely be impacted by how you're paid at your job.

Let's use the example of a 30-year, $200,000 fixed-rate mortgage with a 7.5-percent interest rate. The monthly payment would be $1,398.43 (excluding taxes and insurance). With biweekly payments, each payment would be half—$699.21 (again excluding taxes and insurance). In one year, the payments would total $16,781.16 if monthly ($1,398.43 times 12) and $18,179.46 if biweekly ($699.21 times 26)—a difference of $1,398.30. By paying biweekly rather than monthly, instead of paying approximately $303,425 in interest over the life of the loan, you'd pay only about $225,321. You'd save over $78,104. You'd also pay off the loan 6.5 years sooner—in 23.5 years instead of 30.

For those who can afford to make the biweekly payments, this can be a very attractive opportunity. Another option is to accept a standard fixed-rate loan that has no pre-payment penalties and to make one or more additional payments toward the principal each year. This strategy too will pay off the loan faster and save you a fortune in interest over the term of the mortgage.

Some companies refer to biweekly mortgage products as "mortgage savings programs." The qualifications are basically the same for this type of loan as for a fixed-rate mortgage.

Words of Wisdom from Mark Giordani

A biweekly mortgage isn't much different than any other mortgage, except that the payments are made more often than once per month. What it boils down to is that if a mortgage payment is made biweekly, that's 26 payments per year, which equates to making 13 monthly payments per year instead of 12. I would not recommend paying extra for a biweekly payment privilege. If a broker or lender is going to charge you extra, consider accepting a traditional fixed-rate mortgage and then making one or more extra payments toward the loan's principal per year on your own. The result in terms of your savings will be basically the same and you will have control over when and whether or not to send in those extra payments.

MORE MORTGAGE OPTIONS FOR PEOPLE WITH LESS THAN PERFECT CREDIT

There are various mortgage options designed for people who have credit histories that are less than perfect or whose incomes are not easily verifiable. These people wouldn't typically qualify for a traditional, fixed-rate mortgage from a local bank or financial institution.

These options relate directly to loan approval requirements and can be applied to a variety of mortgage products, although they're typically used for fixed-rate or adjustable-rate mortgages. As you'll discover, what's required to qualify for each will vary greatly by loan product and lender. These loans could have higher costs and a higher interest rate than for a fixed-rate mortgage offered to someone with an excellent credit score. Be sure to discuss these options with your mortgage broker if you believe you could benefit from one of them in your financial situation. Some of these options are *subprime*, *non-conventional,* or *Alt-A* loans.

Stated-Income/Stated-Assets Mortgages. To qualify you for a mortgage, the lender will rely on financial information that you state is accurate, but you will not be required to furnish proof, such as tax returns, pay stubs or bank statements.

> ### *Words of Wisdom from Mark Giordani*
>
> This type of loan is available to certain qualified borrowers on specific loan scenarios. The borrower does not need to provide any supporting documentation about their income or assets. The borrower literally just states what their income and assets are to the lender. This requires you to make a declaration to the lender that the information you're providing is totally accurate. Depending on your employment situation, requirements for this type of loan will vary. Keep in mind: a lender will verify your employment. If you state you're earning a specific salary for doing a specific job, the lender will also do research to make sure that the income you're declaring is within a reasonable and realistic range. Depending on the loan to value calculation and your credit situation, many lenders won't charge extra for this type of loan, nor will you have to pay a higher rate. A SISA (stated-income/stated-assets) loan can be a real timesaver.

No-Income-Verification Loans. To qualify for this type of mortgage product, the borrower will not need to provide proof of his or her income.

The borrower's credit score and credit history will play a major role in the approval process.

> ### *Words of Wisdom from Mark Giordani*
>
> This type of loan allows the borrower to potentially obtain a loan without having to state their income or prove their income. The approval decision is based primarily on assets owned and the borrower's credit. There are several different categories of no-income-verification loans. Again, as the risk for the lender increases, the rate the borrower will need to pay increases. These days, it is possible to obtain a mortgage without having to prove your income, assets, or employment, as long as you have qualifying credit.

No-Documentation Mortgages. To qualify for this type of loan, the borrower will need to have a qualifying credit history, but will not have to provide proof of income, assets, or employment in conjunction with the mortgage application.

> ### *Words of Wisdom from Mark Giordani*
>
> A lot of people assume that with this type of loan, there is no paperwork involved. That's not the case. There is still an application that needs to be completed. You will still need to provide your name, address, date of birth, Social Security number, and credit information. You will not, however, have to provide any information whatsoever about your assets, employment, or income. You may need to provide information about your current housing situation and how much you pay for rent. This may be verified later by the lender. A no-documentation loan means you don't need to supply a lot of supporting documents, like bank statements or pay stubs. There is still, however, a lot of paperwork involved with this type of loan during the closing itself.
>
> This type of loan is ideal for people who have privacy concerns and don't want to reveal certain information about their finances. For someone with poor credit and who desires a no-documentation loan, there's an entirely separate category of loans referred to as *hard-money loans*. Hard-money lenders primarily look at collateral or the value of the property, not at someone's credit or character. This type of lender typically won't lend more than 65 percent of the property's value. You'll also be required to pay a significantly higher interest rate and other fees.

No-Down-Payment Loans. For people who qualify, there are various mortgage products that require either a very low or no down payment.

> ### *Words of Wisdom from Mark Giordani*
>
> A no-down-payment loan is one that requires absolutely no down payment. This is a 100-percent financed transaction, which has become extremely common these days. There are also loan programs that allow the borrower to receive a financial gift from a relative, for example, to cover their down payment. FHA loans and VA loans typically require little or no down payment. There are many loans that require only $500 of the borrower's own funds to use toward the home purchase. There are even loan programs that will provide the buyer with 103 percent of the property value to help cover closings costs and other fees.
>
> On loans with no down payment or a down payment that's below 20 percent of the purchase price of the home, expect that in some circumstances you will be asked to pay for insurance for the lender in case the loan goes bad. This insurance is known as *PMI* or *private mortgage insurance*. There are many ways to get around this insurance requirement. Find a broker who is an expert in this area and you may be able to save some significant money.

FHA Loans. The Federal Housing Administration (FHA) offers government-insured loans that allow people to purchase property with low down payments. While the FHA is not a lender itself, it encourages lenders to offer loans to people who would otherwise not qualify for mortgages by guaranteeing the lender will be repaid, even if the borrower defaults. This is done by requiring the borrower to purchase special mortgage insurance (called a *mortgage insurance premium, MIP*). An estimate for the monthly cost of this added (required) insurance can be calculated by multiplying the loan amount by .5 and then dividing that number by 12. These MIP fees typically last for about seven years. MIP is similar to the private mortgage insurance (PMI) required for other types of loans.

Initially, FHA home loans were for first-time home buyers; however, they're not only for this purpose. Instead of requiring a 20-percent down payment, an FHA loan requires a down payment of three percent of the purchase price, which is much more affordable because the initial cash required to close the loan is lower.

There are set loan limits for FHA loans that vary by region. To learn more, visit the FHA's Web site (at *www.hud.gov*) or discuss this option with your mortgage broker.

> ### *Words of Wisdom from Mark Giordani*
> FHA loans are being insured by the Federal Housing Administration. Because the government is willing to bear some of the risk for the loans, lenders are willing to offer easier credit and income qualifications. These tend to be a little more complex and lengthier to apply for, because a number of government forms also need to be completed. Depending on the circumstances, this type of loan can save borrowers money. In other situations, however, the loan limits may not be high enough to cover the purchase price of a home in certain geographic areas. A good mortgage broker will be able to help you determine if an FHA loan would be a better alternative than another type of loan and step you through the process.

Interest-Only Mortgages. In recent years, this has become a popular mortgage product among homebuyers, because it allows people to purchase more expensive homes without dramatically increasing their monthly payments. This type of loan is more suitable for people who expect their income to increase significantly in the future or who expect the value of their property to increase significantly over time.

With this mortgage product, the monthly payment is only for the interest; no part of it goes toward paying back the principal. Thus, unless the property increases in value, no equity is ever built up. If the value of the property decreases and the borrower wants to sell it, he or she could wind up owing money.

For this type of loan, a five- or ten-year interest-only period is standard. After this period, the principal is then amortized for the remaining term of the loan. Thus, if a borrower had a 30-year mortgage and paid interest only for the first ten years, at the end of that initial period the principal would be amortized for the remaining 20 years. A borrower who expects his or her income to increase can borrow more than he or she could otherwise afford, because monthly payments are lower than for a typical fixed-rate mortgage.

Like all non-traditional mortgage products, this one has pros and cons that you should review with a financial planner or broker. Interest-only loans are not suitable for everyone.

One common option is a more traditional type of loan that allows the borrower to make interest-only payments instead of full payments during months when money is tight. This gives homeowners an extra level of financial flexibility and the ability to better manage periodic unexpected expenses.

SMART-DEBT STRATEGY

If you go with an interest-only loan, don't base your financial decision on the hope that the property will appreciate over time so you'll build equity. You don't want to gamble on the possibility that real estate market values and mortgage rates will improve during the life of the loan. If rates drop or local real estate values drop, you could wind up losing money when you try to sell the home.

Words of Wisdom from Mark Giordani

Interest-only loans are a relatively new mortgage product. For the right borrower, they can be ideal. An interest-only loan has the potential to be riskier than other types of mortgages, but they also have many advantages which you should discuss with your broker.

This type of loan can be excellent if real estate prices are on the rise, because even though you're not building up equity in the home based on your monthly payments, you are building up equity if the value of the property increases. This type of loan is excellent for someone who doesn't have a steady income, who has a seasonal income, or who tends to be paid through commissions. With this type of loan, the borrower always has the option to pay toward the principal of the loan and build equity at any time.

If you utilize this type of loan, make sure you fully understand the terms. Interest-only loans are often associated with ARMs, as opposed to fixed-rate mortgages. There are, however, fixed-rate loans available that have an interest-only option, but expect to pay more in interest for this feature.

One other advantage of an interest-only loan is something called 'recasting' [adjusting the mortgage]. If you take out a $200,000 fixed-rate loan, your monthly payment stays the same for the life of the loan—whether or not you pay any extra toward the principal balance.

With an interest-only loan, one nice feature is that if you are able to pay down the principal balance in an accelerated way, your monthly payments will reflect those payments, in most case, right away. So, as you are paying it down, your payments get lower. This can be a great feature for lots of borrowers who get their income in large payments or bonuses. With all loans, especially interest-only loans and ARMs, you must make every effort to understand what you are getting.

If you take out a five-year interest-only loan, for example, your rate and payments would be fixed for five years. After the fifth year, however, your payment could go up if interest rates go up. Also, the entire principal balance of the loan will now have to be paid off over a 25-year payment schedule. This can mean sharp increases in the payments you need to make just a few years down the road.

I would also suggest that first-time borrowers exercise caution with a new category of loans, called 'option loans,' 'pay option ARMS,' or 'pick-a-payment loans.' These loans traditionally offer three or four different monthly payment option scenarios. If used irresponsibly they can result in losing equity in your home. If you are offered a loan that features multiple payment options, including one payment option that doesn't even cover the monthly interest due, investgate fully.

VA Loans. The Department of Veterans Affairs (VA) offers mortgage opportunities to veterans of the U.S. military. This program, in effect since 1944, allows qualified borrowers to purchase a home with no down payment whatsoever. In other words, this program enables 100-percent financing. VA loans are available to enlisted service personnel with continuous service for a specified number of days (depending on when the person served), a veteran with an honorable discharge, and a surviving spouse of an enlisted soldier killed in the line of duty. Some Reservists also qualify. The amount that can be borrowed varies by region. These loans apply only to single- or multi-family homes that the owner will occupy. Most VA loans are 15- or 30-year fixed-rate mortgages.

For additional information about VA loans, speak with a mortgage broker who specializes in this type of home financing option or visit the VA Web site (*www.homelons.va.gov*)

Words of Wisdom from Mark Giordani

Some VA loans are offered at very good rates and terms. They offer an excellent opportunity for veteran borrowers. The thing about VA loans is that there are not as many different mortgage product types available. In some cases, a non-VA loan may be better suited for a borrower. VA loans require extra paperwork and often take longer to process and get approved than other types of loans.

Assumable Loans. This can be attractive if the person you're buying the home from has a very low interest rate associated with the loan that you could not necessarily qualify for yourself. If you take over the seller's mortgage (assume their loan), you will be responsible to pay the difference between the remaining balance owed on the loan and the asking price (or negotiated selling price) of the home. This difference would need to be made as a down payment.

This is a mortgage that can be transferred from one person to another: the person taking over the loan assumes the liability for it and becomes responsible for making the monthly payments. An assumable loan can be attractive if the seller has a very low interest rate for which you could not necessarily qualify. If you assume a mortgage, you will be responsible for making a down payment of the difference between the balance owed on the loan and the selling price of the home.

Only mortgages that include an *assumption clause* can be assumed. In most cases, ARM loans are assumable, while fixed-rate loans are not.

Words of Wisdom from Mark Giordani

Assumable loans aren't really an entirely separate type of loan, but are more of a feature that some loans include. The advantage is that if you sell the home, a new, qualified buyer may be able to take over the loan without having to refinance it. If an assumable loan is something that is extremely important to you, make sure the terms of the assumability are in writing and are exactly what you anticipated.

Some Pointers on Points

A point is equal to one percent of the mortgage amount. For a $100,000 loan, for example, one point would be $1,000. Paying points on a loan at the closing reduces the interest rate. A one-point loan, for example, will have a lower interest rate than a zero-point loan. Points paid to reduce the interest rate are called *discount points*. The money you pay for points is in addition to your down payment, not part of it.

In deciding whether or not to pay points on a loan, you should consider how long you plan to keep the property and whether or not you can recoup the amount you pay in points if you sell the property or refinance the loan within several years. As a general rule, it doesn't make sense to pay points on a loan if you plan on keeping that loan for less than four years.

Because lenders allow you to choose among rate-and-point combinations for the same loan product, the Mortgage101.com Web site (*www.mortgage101.com*) recommends, "When comparing rates from different lenders, make sure you compare the associated points and rate combinations of the offered program. The published annual percentage rate (APR) is a tool used to compare different terms, offered rates, and points among different lenders and programs."

It's important to note that some lenders charge points as part of their loan-origination fee.

Refinancing 101

Refinancing is the process of replacing a mortgage on a property with another mortgage with different terms. Despite the time and effort it takes to find a lender or broker, shop around for the best deal, choose a mortgage product, complete the application process, provide the necessary paperwork and forms to the lender, and participate in the closing, there are many reasons why you might want to refinance now or in the future. In fact, between the time you buy your home and either sell it or pay off the mortgage, you might opt to refinance more than once as situations change.

In order to refinance, you'll need to qualify all over again and go through virtually the same mortgage application process as the first time. You can dramatically improve your chances of being approved for a lower interest rate and better terms on your new mortgage if:

- You credit score has improved since you obtained your mortgage.
- You've made all of your monthly mortgage payments on time.
- Your income has increased since you obtained your mortgage.
- You've built up equity in your home.
- You plan to refinance a lower principal.
- You can reduce the costs of refinancing, which is easier if you have excellent credit.

There are ways to save money when you refinance, if you take the time to crunch the numbers, fully understand the terms of the new loan, consider the costs associated with refinancing, and then shop around for the very best deal you qualify for. No matter what type of mortgage you have now, your monthly payment is determined primarily by the following factors:

- The principal
- The interest rate
- The length
- The terms
- Fees you paid in conjunction with the loan, including closing costs

Smart Debt Principles and Mortgages

When you refinance, the closing costs and most other fees associated with refinancing can probably be built into the new loan to save you out-of-pocket expenses at the closing. You will likely, however, need to pay for the appraisal in advance. For a typical single-family home, an appraisal will cost between $250 and $350, depending on your geographic area.

If, in refinancing, you can change one or more of the above factors in your favor, such as lowering your interest rate, you could potentially lower your monthly payment and/or save on interest over the life of the loan. Whether you decrease your principal, get a lower interest rate, or change your loan duration, the smallest reductions result in significant savings over the life of the loan.

You may hear from friends or co-workers around the water cooler that it's important to wait for interest rates to drop by at least two percent before you refinance if you hope to save money. This isn't necessarily so. Instead, focus on what the potential new loan offers, the costs associated with it, and the time it'll take to break even, compared with how long you plan to keep the home. Every situation is different. Refinance only if it makes financial sense and you're able to achieve your goals.

As you consider your refinancing options, think carefully about your goals. What are you trying to do? Lower your monthly payment? Shorten the term of the loan? Cash out on the equity in your home? If your current financial situation is very strong, you might want to use your good credit, the equity in your home, and your current income to invest in additional real estate. If, however, times are tough financially, you could refinance in order to obtain some cash. When crunching the numbers to see if refinancing makes sense, knowing how long you intend to own the property can also become a factor, especially if you'll be getting an adjustable-rate mortgage.

SMART-DEBT STRATEGY

Calculate all of the additional fees and closing costs associated with refinancing and then calculate how long it will take you to break even and start saving money. If your plan is to sell or refinance again in just a few months or years, refinancing might not save you money.

As you shop for the best refinancing deals, determine whether any of the mortgage products available could potentially save you more money. For example, you could go from one fixed-rate loan to another, or go from a fixed-rate loan to an adjustable-rate loan, or switch to some other type of mortgage product.

Depending on what you're trying to accomplish and your ability to qualify for approval, your refinancing options will vary greatly. Knowing your goals will help you and your lender/mortgage broker determine your best options.

WATCH OUT FOR PREPAYMENT PENALTIES

By paying off the loan early, the borrower saves money in interest—which would be income for the lender. So, some lenders build prepayment penalties into their mortgages in order to deter the borrower from refinancing or paying off the debt before the term ends.

If your mortgage has a prepayment penalty and you choose to refinance, you could be charged extra to do so. When shopping for a mortgage, look for products that contain absolutely no prepayment penalty. Some loans have a prepayment penalty for only the first few years of the loan. If possible, avoid these too. You never know when your financial situation or interest rates will change dramatically, enabling you to refinance at a better rate and with more attractive terms. If your loan has no prepayment penalty, you have more options.

Not all prepayment penalties are created equal! Just because a loan has a prepayment penalty, that doesn't mean you should necessarily walk away. Discuss with your broker or lender the specifics of any prepayment penalty.

POPULAR REASONS WHY PEOPLE CHOOSE TO REFINANCE

There are many reasons why homeowners refinance. Your reason(s) will help determine which mortgage products best suit your needs. Once again, it's important to sit down with several lenders or mortgage brokers in order to review your current situation and determine what options are available to you for refinancing or cashing out on the equity in your home. If there are any additional expenses, such as closing costs or a cash-out, the refi is called an *equity take-out* or *cash-out refinance*.

Here's some information about some of the most popular reasons why homeowners choose to refinance.

Obtain a Lower Interest Rate. Interest rates offered by lenders change daily. The rate you qualified for when you were approved for your current mortgage was based on a variety of factors. If interest rates have gone down in general, even by a fraction of a point, it might make sense to refinance in order to reduce your monthly payment and the amount of money you'll be paying in interest over the life of the loan.

Smart Debt Principles and Mortgages

Here's an example. If you have a $200,000, 30-year, fixed-rate mortgage at 7.25 percent, your monthly payment is $1,364.35 and the interest over the 30 years is $291,166.

If interest rates drop to 6.75 percent, for the same $200,000 30-year, fixed-rate mortgage, your monthly payment would be $1,297.20 and the interest you'd pay would be $266,992. So, not only would your monthly payment drop by $67.15 per month, you'd save $24,174 in interest. But wait, there's more! If you've been paying off your mortgage on time for five years, for example, your outstanding principal would be lower than the $200,000 you borrowed. You could now refinance that lower amount for either a full 30 years (which would lower your payment even more) or only 25 years (or less). So, you could save in interest plus cut the term of your mortgage.

Use an amortization calculator, like the one at *finance.realtor.com/HomeFinance/calculators/mortgagepayment.asp*, to calculate the financial benefits of refinancing a fixed-rate mortgage. You can also find online calculators that'll help you determine if refinancing with another type of loan makes more financial sense in your situation. Ideally, however, you should talk with at least one mortgage broker or lender who can review your refinancing options based on current interest rates.

Even if interest rates in general have not dropped, you can still refinance and benefit from a lower interest rate in one of several ways. First, if your credit score has improved since you obtained your mortgage, chances are you'd now qualify for a lower interest rate, especially if you've built up equity in your home and you've made all of your mortgage payments on time. Second, if you refinance, you can pay points to lower your interest rate. Third, you could potentially switch from a fixed-rate mortgage to an adjustable-rate mortgage that offers lower rates and better terms. If there's a way to decrease your interest rate, even by a fraction of a point, the benefits of refinancing could be dramatic.

Get Better Terms on the Mortgage. When refinancing, you can adjust the terms of your mortgage or potentially save money by switching mortgage products altogether. You could go from a fixed-rate mortgage to some type of adjustable-rate mortgage or an interest-only mortgage, for example.

By switching to an adjustable-rate mortgage (with an initial fixed-rate period), you could probably get a more attractive interest rate, which would save you money. You'd run the risk, however, that after the fixed-rate period your interest rate could rise significantly. You could possibly avoid this increase by refinancing again down the road, but you could lose out over the long term if interest rates rise significantly or you have to pay high closing costs each time. Before choosing this refinancing option, consider how long you'll be in your home. If you know you'll be moving in four years, for example, you can refinance now with an ARM that has a fixed-rate period of five years and benefit from the savings with no risk of a higher rate after that period, because you'll be moving or selling the home. Of course, consult with your lender or broker to see if this scenario works for you.

Different mortgage products and different lenders and brokers offer vastly different terms, which is why it's important to evaluate your needs and shop around for the best deal. If you want to save money by refinancing, even a subtle change in the interest rate, the duration, or the terms could make a significant difference.

Cut or Reset the Term of the Mortgage. Whether or not you can qualify for a lower interest rate, you can still benefit financially if you can refinance at better terms. One way to do this is to refinance for a shorter term. If you go from a 30-year fixed-rate loan to a 25-year or 20-year fixed-rate loan, your savings in interest over the life of the loan will be dramatic. If you can get a lower rate when you reduce the term of the mortgage, you could potentially decrease your monthly payment as well.

For example, if you started with a 20-year fixed-rate mortgage and have been paying it off for ten years, you could now refinance at the same or even a higher interest rate, but set the length of the new loan back to 20 or more years. This would *not* save you money (in fact, it would cost you more), but it would lower your monthly payment, which might help you address current financial shortfalls or problems.

Cash out on the Equity in Your Home. If you made a down payment when you purchased your home, that amount immediately established equity. Since then, if you've been paying off some of your mortgage principal with each monthly payment, you've been slowly building equity. Finally, if the appraised value of your home has increased since you purchased it, the difference between its current value and your purchase price also represents equity in your home.

Regardless of which mortgage product you use to refinance, the lender will almost always require you to maintain at least some equity in your home, at least ten to 25 percent. However, there are exceptions. There are some refinancing options that allow you to refinance for more than 100 percent of the home's appraised value, but you must have excellent credit and meet other requirements to obtain this type of loan.

As long as you have equity in your home and meet the qualification guidelines of the lenders, you can borrow against or cash out on your equity in order to obtain cash. Doing this would increase the amount you owe on your mortgage (or other types of loans, such as a home equity line of credit), but you could access cash quickly.

Here are some of the most popular reasons why people opt to cash out on some or all of their equity:

- Make home improvements
- Pay for school or college tuition
- Consolidate and pay off high-interest debt, such as credit cards
- Finance a divorce settlement
- Pay medical expenses not covered by health insurance
- Purchase a big-ticket item, such as an expensive car or boat
- Invest in another property, such as a vacation home or investment property

Typically, tapping the equity in your home for a significant amount of money is ultimately cheaper than using a high-interest credit card or taking out some other type of loan. Plus, there are certain tax advantages, since the interest you pay on your home loan is tax-deductible, while the interest you pay on other types of unsecured loans is not deductible.

In some rare situations, instead of refinancing your mortgage, the lender will allow you to modify your loan. *Loan modification* is most common when the borrower wants to keep all of the terms of the loan identical, but can now put a large sum of money toward the principal, which will lower the monthly payments.

When you decide to refinance in order to cash out on your equity, your options will depend on your credit history and your ability to meet the eligibility and approval requirements of the various lenders and brokers.

See Chapter 4 for information about other ways to tap into your equity without having to refinance your primary mortgage. You'll learn how to apply smart-debt principles when obtaining a second mortgage, a home equity loan, or a home equity line of credit (HELOC).

SMART-DEBT STRATEGY

Do you want to learn more about this topic? Pick up copies of these two *Entrepreneur Magazine's Personal Finance Pocket Guides* books by Jason R. Rich: *Why Rent? Own Your Dream Home!* and *Mortgages and Refinancing: Get The Best Rates.*

THE PAPERWORK YOU'LL NEED TO REFINANCE

Once you decide to refinance, you'll want to gather pertinent information about your current mortgage and financial situation. This includes reacquainting yourself with the terms of your mortgage. As you start talking with lenders and brokers about refinancing, early on in the application process you'll need to provide the following information, in addition to the information you'd need to provide if you were buying a home and shopping for a mortgage:

- The current value of your home (an appraisal will be ordered by the lender or broker)
- The current amount owed on your mortgage
- The interest rate and terms of the current mortgage
- Your credit history and credit score (the broker or lender will order copies of your credit reports and obtain your credit scores)

During the refinancing application process, be prepared to provide the lender or broker with your pay stubs from the last 30 days, copies of W-2 forms for the past two years (or tax returns for the same period, depending on your employment situation), two months' worth of bank statements, two months' worth of statements for your investment and IRA accounts, and information about your employment and housing for the past two years. You'll also need to provide copies of your current mortgage documents, which you received at the closing. To save time and avoid unnecessary delays, start gathering these documents early in the refinancing process.

CHAPTER 4 | Smart Debt Principles and Second Mortgages, Home Equity Loans, and Home Equity Lines of Credit

*T*his chapter is for people who own a home (with or without a mortgage) and who are looking to cash out on some of the equity they have in their property. This can be an intelligent financial strategy, if it's done correctly and for the right reasons. Common reasons why people choose to cash out on their equity will be covered shortly, as will some of the options beyond refinancing.

In addition to using home financing appropriately to meet your specific goals, you'll once again also want to apply basic smart-debt principles. Let's review some of the smart-debt principles from the previous chapter and build on this list to accommodate the additional debt you'll be taking on if you choose to cash out on the equity in your home by taking out a second mortgage, a home equity loan, or a home equity line of credit.

Smart-debt principles to consider:

1. Establish a credit history and a credit score that allow you to obtain a prime rate or "A paper" loan. You want your score to be at least 620; a score in the mid- to-high 700s is ideal.

2. Determine exactly how you want to use the cash you receive and how much you'll need. Then, create a plan for spending it intelligently. Borrow only the money you need, when you need it. (The exception to this is if you'll be using a home equity line of credit.) Even if you qualify for a larger loan than you need, don't take it unless you have a good reason.

3. Find a home financing product with the lowest rates and fees for which you qualify, based on your credit history, credit score, employment/income, etc.

4. Work with a knowledgeable, reputable, and experienced mortgage broker or lender. Negotiate for the lowest fees.

5. Develop a detailed plan for making the monthly payments to repay the loan in a timely manner. The longer you maintain the outstanding debt, the more it will cost you in interest and potential fees.

6. Crunch the numbers and make sure that after you pay all of the closing costs, fees, and interest on this new debt, you'll still meet your original objectives, especially if you're consolidating other debts.

7. Make sure you can't meet your financial needs and goals by simply refinancing your mortgage, as opposed to taking on a second mortgage, a home equity loan, or a home equity line of credit and probably paying a slightly higher interest rate. To make this determination, consider how much money you need, when you need the money, how long you need the money, and how you'll be spending the money.

Methods of Cashing out on the Equity in Your Home

As you know, a mortgage allows you to borrow a significant amount of money to buy real estate using your home as collateral. Once you build up equity in your home, it's possible to borrow against that equity, again using your home as collateral. If you default on your mortgage, on a home equity loan, or on a home equity line of credit, the bank or lender can initiate a foreclosure, causing you to lose your home.

If you decide to cash out on your home's equity, there are several ways to do this.

First, you can refinance your mortgage. The new mortgage would be for a higher amount than you owe on your current mortgage, allowing you to receive the difference in cash. For example, if your home is appraised at $200,000 and you owe $150,000 on your mortgage, you have $50,000 in equity. When you refinance, the principal of your new mortgage could be $175,000, enabling you to receive $25,000 in cash (not taking into account fees, closing costs, taxes, etc.), yet still retain $25,000 of equity in your home.

The benefit to this is that you receive cash at a lower interest rate than if you were to take out an unsecured loan or use your credit cards, for example. Plus, there are tax advantages, because the interest you pay on your mortgage is tax-deductible, while the interest you pay on other types of loans is not.

In the previous chapter, you learned about refinancing. This chapter explores three other popular ways homeowners can tap into the equity in their home in order to receive cash:

- a second mortgage
- a home equity line of credit
- a home equity loan

A *second mortgage* works just like a regular mortgage, but it remains totally separate from your first mortgage—with its own rate and terms. Your home equity is used as collateral. The lender for the second mortgage is not entitled to any proceeds from the sale of the home until the lender on the first mortgage has been repaid. Because the lender of the second mortgage carries added risks, rates tend to be higher than for a first mortgage.

A *home equity loan* is a loan with a specified term at a fixed rate of interest, using your house as collateral. Just as with a fixed-rate mortgage, your monthly payment on a home equity loan remains the same. Interest rates on home equity loans are typically higher than for mortgages, but lower than for other types of loans, such as credit cards or car loans. A home equity loan has tax benefits, but they're more limited than with a mortgage. Typically, from a tax standpoint, borrowers can deduct interest on home equity loans only up to $100,000. The money you receive through a home equity loan can be used for almost anything, such as home improvements, debt consolidation, medical expenses, the purchase of big-ticket items, or school tuition.

A *home equity line of credit (HELOC)* is a type of second mortgage. It provides the borrower with a firm commitment from the lender to make a specified amount of funds available for a specified period of time, using the equity in his or her home as collateral. The difference between a HELOC and a home equity loan is that a HELOC is flexible: during the term of the loan agreement, the borrower can borrow any amount of money up to the credit limit at any time and as often as he or she wants and pay back the outstanding balance over time. HELOCs also differ from home equity loans in that the interest rate is adjustable, not fixed, and the interest is calculated daily. A HELOC has an annual fee. This type of loan can be used as a financial safety net that a homeowner taps only when and if it's needed. This type of loan works more like a credit card than a mortgage.

What's unique about these types of loans is that the amount you're able to borrow is almost always directly related to the equity you already have in your home. Especially if the real estate market is good and local property values have been on the rise, you may discover you possess more equity in your home than you thought.

When you purchased the home, the down payment you made (the amount of the purchase price you didn't finance) established equity right from the start. For example, if you purchased a $200,000 home with a $170,000 mortgage and a $30,000 down payment, immediately after your closing you had $30,000 of equity in your home. If you've been paying off your mortgage month after month and part of each payment has gone toward the loan's principal, that's how much has been building your equity. So, after five years of paying your mortgage (depending on the terms of your mortgage), you may have built up an additional $10,000 to $15,000 or more in equity.

Now, if the appraised value of your home has gone up, that increase is also considered equity. Thus, if you paid $200,000 for the home, but it's now worth $350,000, your equity has increased by $150,000. This is equity you can borrow against and turn into cash that can be used for a wide range of purposes.

Decisions in Choosing a Loan or a Line of Credit

Your broker or lender will be able to help you decide whether refinancing your mortgage, obtaining a second mortgage, obtaining a home equity loan, or obtaining a HELOC is most suitable to meet your needs, based on your current financial situation, credit score, and objectives.

> ### SMART-DEBT STRATEGY
>
> The ideal smart-debt approach is to tap into equity in your home using the least expensive method possible that will enable you to achieve your financial goals.

In order to get reliable advice, you'll need to provide your lender or broker with accurate information and a summary of your goals. You'll need to answer at least the following questions:

- How much money do you need?
- How will you use the money?
- Do you need the money in one lump sum?
- Can you afford an additional monthly payment? If so, how much?
- Do you want a fixed rate or are you comfortable with a variable rate?
- How long will you need the money? Over what period of time do you plan to pay it back?

In order to apply smart-debt principles, you'll want to ask yourself these additional questions:

- How will you pay back the money? Will taking on the additional monthly payment negatively impact your quality of life or your ability to meet your other financial obligations?
- What is your backup plan if you run into unforeseen financial problems later?
- Does taking on this additional debt help you meet your financial goals? If so, how? If you're consolidating your debt, for example, how much money will you ultimately be saving and over what time period?
- After you crunch the numbers, does taking on this additional debt make financial sense in your unique situation?
- Do you understand exactly how the loan works, what your obligations are, what your liability is, and what your monthly payments will be after all closing costs and fees are calculated?
- Have you discussed the potential tax advantages of this loan with your accountant or financial planner? Does the loan option you're choosing really make the most sense for you?
- How much will adding this debt cost you over time? Is there a cheaper way to do it?

Once you've reviewed your situation with a lender or broker and pinpointed your needs, shop around for the best rates, just as you would for a traditional mortgage. Then, once you decide what type of loan you want, be prepared for an application-and-approval process that's very similar to applying for a mortgage. There will be plenty of paperwork to complete, plus you'll need to provide financial documentation, such as W-2s, tax returns, bank statements, and pay stubs.

Just as there are many types of mortgage products, each with very different approval guidelines, the same is true for second mortgages, home equity loans, and HELOCs. To qualify for any of these loans, you'll need to meet the approval guidelines of the lender, who will evaluate your income, employment situation, credit history, and credit scores. The lender will also look at how faithful you've been at making the monthly payments on your current mortgage (late payments can hurt your chances) and evaluate your ability to take on the additional debt and make the additional monthly payment(s).

SMART-DEBT STRATEGY

Failure to repay the loans described in this chapter and meet your obligations to the lender can result in foreclosure on your home because it is being used as collateral. If you won't be able to afford the additional monthly payments to repay this debt, don't use it or you could find yourself homeless and in serious financial trouble.

Second Mortgage: Is It Right for You?

A second mortgage works just like a first mortgage. There are many types of mortgage products to choose from, depending on your ability to qualify and your purpose(s). On a second mortgage, however, expect to pay a higher interest rate, because the lender takes on a greater risk regardless of your credit score or credit history. Since the second mortgage uses as collateral property that has already been pledged as collateral for the first mortgage, the rights of the lender of the second mortgage are subordinate to the rights of the lender of the first when it comes to getting any proceeds if the home is sold, for example.

The benefit to this type of loan is that the interest you pay is typically tax-deductible. Plus, you'll be repaying the loan over a long period of time, so the monthly payments tend to be affordable, and the interest rate is lower than if you used a credit card or some other unsecured loan, for example. With this type of loan, you must immediately repay the outstanding balance in full if and when you sell your home.

A second mortgage can be at a fixed rate or an adjustable rate. Qualification requirements vary dramatically based on the lender, your financial situation, and the mortgage product. If, after consulting with a financial planner, accountant, mortgage broker, or lender, you determine that a second mortgage can meet your needs, be sure to shop around for the best rates and terms.

Words of Wisdom from Mark Giordani

As an alternative to high-priced loans from credit cards and other non-secured personal loans, some of my clients prefer the advantages of a second mortgage. Typical uses include paying for school tuition, medical bills, or home improvements, such as adding a garage or an additional room. One thing to look out for with second mortgages is the terms of the loan. Some are written to be fully paid off in 10 years, while others are written to be paid off in 30 years. The shorter the term, the higher the monthly payment.

Generally speaking, second mortgage loans are fixed-rate mortgages and the payments are amortized payments.

One potential drawback to a second mortgage, especially if they're used for a no-points/no-closing-costs refinance transaction, is that the rates may have to be very high to cover all of the costs associated with the lender offering this type of financing. This is especially true with small loan amounts, under $100,000, on second mortgages.

The procedure for applying for a second mortgage is no different than applying for a first mortgage, other than that the lender will use the anticipated monthly payment for the second mortgage when calculating your eligibility for the financing when considering your income.

It's important to understand that a second mortgage can take on the form of a home equity loan or home equity line of credit.

Home Equity Loans: The Pros and Cons

A home equity loan is a type of second mortgage. The borrower receives a single lump sum of money once. The loan has a fixed duration and a fixed interest rate. Thus, the monthly payments remain the same until the debt is repaid. This type of loan can be used for a variety of purposes, such as debt consolidation, home improvements, or a big-ticket item. With this type of loan, you must immediately repay the outstanding balance in full if and when you sell your home.

> ### *Words of Wisdom from Mark Giordani*
> Home equity loans are a great low- or no-cost way of accessing money from the equity in your home. A home equity loan is often a second mortgage behind an existing first mortgage. However, someone who owns their home outright and does not currently possess a mortgage can still obtain a first-position home equity loan, which is the same as a first mortgage.
>
> Depending on the rates and terms of your first mortgage, if applicable, it often works out better to refinance your first mortgage for a larger amount than to take out a second mortgage or home equity loan, especially if there are any costs or fees associated with obtaining the loan. Second mortgages and home equity loans tend to carry higher interest rates and are very dependent upon an accurate property appraisal. The amount you can borrow is limited by your home's current market value, not necessarily what you paid for your home.

A Home Equity Line of Credit: Cash When You Need It

The best thing about a HELOC is that it gives you a specified loan amount that you can use anytime within a specified draw or withdrawal period (typically five to 15 years). The funds are available only if you choose to use them, by writing a check, using a credit card, or making a telephone money transfer.

You can borrow whatever amount you need up to your limit. You can also borrow as many times as you wish within the draw period, although you need to start paying back the loan as soon you begin using the line of credit.

The terms of this type of loan are more like a credit card with an adjustable interest rate and an annual fee. This type of loan can be used for a wide range of purposes.

Here's one example of how you might use this loan. After the line of credit is opened, you're given a limit of $30,000. You then immediately withdraw $10,000 to consolidate your credit card balances and your other debts. You now have to begin repaying that $10,000, but still have $20,000 available. As you pay back the $10,000, your credit line goes back up. This credit line gives you a tremendous amount of flexibility and can save you money if you use it responsibly.

While there are many types of HELOCs and the terms and rates vary greatly, the rates are typically adjustable. The repayment period on a HELOC can be anywhere from five to 30 years and is generally longer than the draw/withdrawal period. Typically, the minimum monthly payment covers only the interest, not the principal. You must repay the outstanding balance in full immediately if and when you sell your home.

SMART-DEBT STRATEGY

To have an extra financial cushion when you need it, it's typically a good strategy to apply for a HELOC and get approved while your credit score is high and after you've been approved for your initial mortgage. You may never have to use the HELOC, but if you have a financial emergency, the money will be available to you immediately when you need it. It's better to apply for this type of loan before you run into any financial problems or emergencies.

Since this type of loan has an adjustable rate, your required monthly payments could rise, even if your income doesn't. Plus, if the value of your home drops when you decide to sell it, you could wind up earning less on the sale than you owe on the loan.

Words of Wisdom from Mark Giordani

In terms of qualifying for a HELOC, the process is the same as applying for a mortgage or home equity loan in terms of the time and paperwork involved. The major advantage of a HELOC is that the balance can go up and down, depending on how you want to use it. It's very flexible, like a credit card, but with generally lower rates than a credit card. Another advantage of a HELOC is that the payment is generally calculated as an interest-only payment, so that for the same amount of money borrowed, a home equity line of credit will have a lower monthly payment than a home equity loan, assuming the interest rate is the same.

A disadvantage of a HELOC is that the interest rate most often is a variable rate that is tied to the prime rate. If the prime rate changes, your monthly payments increase or decrease accordingly. The other disadvantage to a HELOC is that, unlike a credit card, the loan taken against your

---

home is secured by your home. Should you be unable to make the monthly payments, the bank/lender may foreclose on your property. This is not generally the case with credit card debt.

There are some newer HELOC products that do offer fixed rates on the entire balance or some portion thereof. Brokers and lenders sometimes earn their fees based on the amount of money that you actually borrow from the home equity line of credit. If you take out a home equity line for $100,000, do not be surprised if your bank or broker requires you to draw a minimum of approximately $20,000 off the line. In some cases, if you do not draw or use the HELOC, the company that is providing it to you only earns minimal fees and cannot cover the costs of providing a line that goes completely unused. Be sure to discuss draw requirements, annual fees, and early-termination fees with your lender on any home equity line.

It is also essential to know how your interest rate will adjust if you have an adjustable-rate HELOC. The best time to get a HELOC established on your home is when purchasing your home, if you have the equity to qualify. By doing it at that time, you will have access to the line in the event of an emergency. Because you are qualifying for it at the time of getting your first mortgage, it may cost less to obtain and your broker/lender may be able to give you a break on the fees that you would otherwise have to pay. You'll also need to provide your financial documentation only once, so the application process is streamlined.

SMART-DEBT STRATEGY

Using a HELOC or home equity loan to consolidate your debt can potentially save you money on your overall monthly payments. However, over the long term, you may wind up paying more in interest charges, especially if you take 20 or 30 years to repay the loan. It's important to crunch the numbers and calculate your potential savings in the short term and long term before moving forward with any type of loan.

Always Be Responsible with Your Spending

While a second mortgage, home equity loan, or HELOC can make a large sum of cash available to you, this is money that you must pay back—with interest. Spend it responsibly! If you're using the proceeds to consolidate your other debts or to fix some financial mistakes, learn from those mistakes and don't repeat them.

As a homeowner, it's vital that you develop a monthly budget that enables you to live within your means. It's equally important to stick to that budget. If you can't make ends meet now and you're relying on your credit cards or a home equity loan, for example, to pay your basic living expenses, you're simply building up more debt and overspending. If this is the case, adjust your spending habits quickly to avoid long-term financial disaster. At some point, you'll reach the credit limit on your credit cards, spend the equity you have in your home, and deplete your savings. You'll still be responsible for paying off all of your outstanding debt and covering your ongoing basic living expenses. How will you do this?

If you need help establishing a budget, seek the guidance of an accountant (CPA) or financial planner. If you've run into problems with credit, work with a reputable credit counselor to help remedy the situation. Part of being a responsible homeowner involves learning how to deal with the financial responsibilities of owning and maintaining your home.

Unfortunately, while homeowners have many options for taking a smart-debt approach to their living expenses and using the equity in their home, people who rent don't have this opportunity. They have no equity and the rent is set by their landlord. Their only options are to negotiate the best rent possible before signing the lease or to find an alternative place to live that's cheaper.

In the next chapter, we'll focus on applying smart-debt principles to your primary mode of transportation—your vehicle. As you're about to discover, when it comes to what you drive and how you pay for it, you have a wide range of options.

CHAPTER 5 | Applying Smart-Debt Principles to Auto Financing and Leases

*U*nless you live in a major city and can rely exclusively on public transportation and your own two feet to get around, chances are, you'll need to buy or lease a car. Unless you pay for the car outright using cash from your savings, you'll want to apply a handful of smart-debt principles when buying or leasing a car. As you're about to discover, the car-buying or -leasing process involves a lot of decisions. This chapter focuses mainly on the financial decisions.

The first step in buying or leasing a vehicle is to choose the type of vehicle. You've got a wide range of choices, including the following:

- convertible
- hybrid
- mini-passenger van
- sedan (compact, midsize, full-size, or luxury)
- sport utility vehicle (SUV)
- sports car

- station wagon
- truck

Next, you need to narrow down your options by selecting a particular manufacturer (e.g., GM, Honda, Ford, Volvo, BMW, or Hyundai) and then a specific model. Every car manufacturer offers a selection of car models and then allows you to choose options.

After deciding on the specific car, the next step is to decide if you want your vehicle new or used. Then, you'll need to decide whether you'll buy or lease and how you'll pay for it. If you'll be financing the purchase of the vehicle or leasing it, your credit history and credit score will determine whether or not you get approved and what the terms of the financing or lease will be.

Many people base their car-buying or -leasing decision exclusively on the emotional attachment they develop with the vehicle they choose. While it's important to love your ride, it's equally important to make smart financial decisions about acquiring those wheels. Once you choose a make and model of vehicle, invest a little extra time to compare comparable vehicles from other manufacturers. Also, shop around multiple dealerships.

Applying Smart-Debt Principles to Buying or Leasing

The cost of buying or leasing a vehicle can range from three digits to well over $50,000, depending on the make and model. Because this is a rather significant amount of money, applying a handful of smart-debt principles can help you save money.

The following are a few strategies for applying smart-debt principles to the buying or leasing process:

- Work with a reputable and knowledgeable dealership (unless you're buying a used vehicle directly from its current owner).
- Determine exactly how much you can afford and are willing to pay for the vehicle.
- If you'll be financing or leasing the vehicle, determine the highest possible monthly payment you can afford. Don't forget about all of the additional costs you'll incur, including insurance, registration and inspection, gas, maintenance, and taxes. Your auto insurance alone can add several hundred dollars per month to your monthly

expenses, so even if the monthly payment for the vehicle's financing makes sense and fits within your budget, make sure you can afford all of the other costs associated with the vehicle.

- Select a vehicle that makes sense for you, based on your needs and driving habits. Test-drive the car to make sure you find it comfortable and easy to drive. If you'll be mostly commuting to and from work, you probably don't need a gas-guzzling SUV. Choose a vehicle that makes financial sense to drive and maintain, based on how you'll be using the vehicle.

- Research the vehicle's safety, quality, customer satisfaction records, and fuel economy.

- Figure out how much you can expect to pay for gas, maintenance, insurance, etc., based on your driving habits, geographic area, and personal situation. *Consumer Reports* magazine is one resource for researching the safety and repair/maintenance costs of specific makes and models. Another excellent resource is the U.S. Department of Transportation's Auto Safety Hotline (800 424-9393), which provides information about recalls.

- Do research to find the best price for the vehicle of your choice. The Internet is an extremely valuable research tool, both for learning about specific makes and models of vehicles and for exploring your financing options. AutoTrader.com, Vehix.com, and Cars.com are all excellent, general-interest car-related Web sites. You can also visit the Web sites of car manufacturers, such as GM (*www.gm.com*), Honda (*www.honda.com*), BMW (*www.bmw.com*), Volvo (*www.volvo.com*), and Hyundai (*www.hyundai-motor.com*), for example, to learn about each model available from each manufacturer.

- Choose the options and accessories you want and determine how these additions impact the cost of the vehicle. Also take into account the cost of a service contract if you plan on purchasing one from the dealership.

- Negotiate the vehicle price with the dealership or current owner. Determine which makes more financial sense—to trade in your current vehicle or to sell it yourself.

- Choose a financing, leasing, or payment option that makes the most sense for you, based on your personal situation. Shop around for the best financing options that you qualify for. In addition to working with the dealership, there are other financing options you can pursue, such as an auto loan from a bank or credit union. You could also use a home equity loan or a HELOC if it makes better financial sense in your situation.

SMART-DEBT STRATEGY

Most car dealerships work with multiple lenders and can help customers obtain a loan almost regardless of their credit score. But the deal you're offered if your credit score is below average won't be competitive. To keep the monthly payment reasonable, the lender may extend the loan to 60 months (five years), for example. This could be a problem: if the vehicle lasts only three to four years, based on the quality of the car, your driving habits, and how well you maintain it, you could wind up upside-down on the loan when you attempt to sell it. This means that you would owe more on the car than it's worth if you were to trade it in or sell it. So, if you still owe $10,000 on the car, but it's worth only $8,500 if you sell it, you'd still have to pay $1,500 out-of-pocket to get rid of the car. This is not a situation you want to be in!

Especially if finances are tight, find a car that you know will last you three to five years and then don't accept a car loan that goes beyond that length of time. Unless it's absolutely necessary, get a loan for three years, not five. This will not only save you money in interest and allow you to own the car outright much sooner. It'll also help to prevent you from being upside-down on the loan when you attempt to sell the vehicle.

Don't focus just on the monthly payment, especially if you're financing the vehicle. Concentrate first on negotiating the best possible purchase price for the vehicle; then focus on finding the best financing option available. How much will the loan cost you in interest over time? That's a matter of the annual percentage rate (APR) and the length of the loan. The APR will be determined, in large part, based on your credit score. So, work on the length of the loan.

Finally, at some dealerships, in order to obtain financing or to receive a competitive APR, you may, depending on your credit score, be required to pay a sizable down payment.

Before you sign a contract to purchase, finance, or lease any vehicle, review all of the terms carefully and make sure you understand your obligations. All of the blanks on the contract should be properly filled in before you sign it.

Same Car, Same Dealer, Different Price— Go Figure!?

To help convince you to purchase or lease a vehicle, many car dealers will make it sound as if they're offering you an amazing deal. But in reality, not only is the dealership making a fortune from the sale, but the lending company will also be making a significant profit by providing you with the loan. It may sound like a great deal to be paying $500 less than the car's sticker price, but you could probably do much better!

The following terms will help you understand what the salesperson is talking about and what's actually being offered to you.

- **Invoice price**—This is what the manufacturer charges the dealership for the vehicle. The invoice price is typically higher than what the dealer actually pays, because the dealership often receives rebates, discounts, allowances, and other types of incentive rewards that consumers are not told about. Determine if the invoice price includes the destination and delivery charge the dealership pays. If so, make sure you don't pay it twice. To figure out what the dealerships are really paying for vehicles—and to determine how much profit they're making—you'll probably need to pay for car pricing information offered by Edmunds (*www.edmunds.com*), CarPrice.com (*www.carprice.com*), or *Kelley Blue Book* (*www.kbb.com*). You can also find this information in guides published by *Consumer Reports* and *Kelley Blue Book,* available at your local bookstore or newsstand. When you begin negotiating, focus on the invoice price (or the price you know the dealer paid for the vehicle), not the sticker price.
- **Base price**—This is the price of the vehicle without any added options. This price should include all standard equipment and the factory warranty. After you've added the options you want, the price will typically be much higher.
- **Sticker price**—This is the price of the vehicle that by law must be displayed on a label in the vehicle's window. It shows the base price and lists (separately) the manufacturer's installed options. It also shows the destination and delivery charge and the manufacturer's suggested retail price (MSRP). On this same sticker, you'll find the vehicle's fuel economy (mileage). The sticker price is the asking price for the vehicle. However, you can negotiate it down.

Financing Options

When you purchase a vehicle, you have two basic choices. You can pay cash and buy it outright or you can finance the purchase. If you finance, the dealer will almost always help you. At the dealership, you'll fill out a complete loan application and give permission for the dealer and potential lenders to access your credit report and credit score. The dealer may submit your application to multiple lenders in order to qualify you for financing.

Before this happens, check your credit score and determine approximately what interest rate you qualify for on a car loan. (Your credit rating and score may not qualify you for the rates advertised in car ads. You can determine approximately what type of financing deals you'll qualify for, based on your credit score and geographic area, by visiting the Bankrate.com Web site (*www.bankrate.com*).

If your credit score is average or better, you may be able to save money by taking out the loan through a local bank, credit union, or other financial institution. You can also shop around for the best deal: you can do research and even apply for a car loan via the Internet.

If your credit score is below average, it will often make sense to find someone with a higher credit score who will cosign for the loan. With a cosigner, you will be offered a more attractive financing deal. The cosigner shares responsibility for paying off the loan, which will also appear on his or her credit report.

SMART-DEBT STRATEGY

Just like when shopping for a mortgage, when you shop around for car financing, the credit bureaus give you a 30-day period during which any number of dealers and lenders can check your credit report and the multiple inquiries will count as only one inquiry on your credit report.

Once you decide you'll be financing your vehicle, here is some advice for determining if you're receiving the best financing deal possible. Remember: when shopping around for a deal, it's always a good strategy to contact at least three lenders.

1. Determine the exact price you'll be paying for the vehicle. This is the final price after your negotiations are completed and all of the options and add-ons have been calculated into the price.

2. Determine the exact amount you'll be financing. This will be the final price of the vehicle, minus your down payment.
3. Determine the value of the car you'll be trading in, if you decide to do so. If you sell your car yourself, you'll almost always get more than if you trade it in on a new car. Do some research on what it's worth. Use the value of the trade as part of your negotiation strategy.
4. Determine the interest rate (APR) being offered and calculate how much the purchase will actually cost you over the term of the loan. The longer the term, the more interest you'll pay, but the lower your monthly payment will be. The APR will be determined by a number of factors, including your credit score, current finance rates, market conditions, and special financing offers from manufacturers and/or lenders.
5. Determine the duration of the loan, the number of monthly payments, and the amount of the payment.
6. Figure out if you can really afford the monthly payment and other costs—insurance, licensing, gas, maintenance, and any local taxes. You do not want to lose the vehicle because six months or two years down the road you find that you can't afford the payments. A repossession will be listed on your credit report and stay there for seven years. This will make it much more difficult for you to buy or lease a vehicle.

After you have determined all of the facts, you can shop around for the best financing deal possible for your credit score. When you see ads for 0 percent financing or other incentives to buy a specific make and model of car, keep in mind that these offers are given only to people with excellent credit. If your credit score is below the mid-700s, you will probably not qualify for the special financing or cash-back offers being advertised. In addition to working with the dealership's financing department, contact one or more local banks, credit unions, or lenders for competitive financing deals.

Let's compare three- and five-year loans with different APRs and terms, so you can see how the monthly payment will vary. For these examples, let's assume that the final negotiated price of the vehicle is $24,000. (These examples do not take into account sales tax or a trade-in.)

The duration of a car loan can be 36 months, 48 months, 60 months, or even 72 months. From a smart-debt standpoint, it seldom makes sense to take on a car loan for 72 months, especially if there's a good chance you won't be driving that car in six years. While it is possible to refinance a car loan, you often won't receive the best rates available. However, you might consider consolidating your loan if you refinance your mortgage or take out a home equity loan, for example; this could save you money in interest and provide tax advantages.

	36 Months	60 Months
Final Purchase Price	$24,000	$24,000
10% Down Payment	$2,400	$2,400
Amount Financed	$21,600	$21,600
APR	6%	6%
Monthly Payment	$657.11	$417.58
Total Price (with interest)	$26,056	$27,455

Example #1. Three years and five years at 6 percent

Example #1 demonstrates the difference in your monthly payment and total vehicle price if your credit score is above average and qualifies you for a 6 percent APR. (If your credit score is excellent, you could qualify for an even more competitive APR—possibly even 0 percent.)

In terms of using smart debt, it makes much more sense to finance the vehicle at 6 percent for three years and pay a total of $26,056 than to finance the vehicle for five years at 12 percent and pay $31,228 (Example #3). If you can afford the higher monthly payment, it will cost you less down the road. Adopting a smart-debt approach means looking at long-term saving possibilities.

	36 Months	60 Months
Final Purchase Price	$24,000	$24,000
10% Down Payment	$2,400	$2,400
Amount Financed	$21,600	$21,600
APR	8%	8%
Monthly Payment	$676.86	$437.97
Total Price (with interest)	$26,767	$28,678

Example #2. Three years and five years at 8 percent

SMART DEBT

In Example #2, at an 8 percent APR, if you obtained a three-year loan, your monthly payment would be $676.86 and you'd wind up spending $26,767 on the vehicle by the time you paid off the loan. If you took out this same loan for five years, your monthly payment would drop to $437.97, but you'd be paying $28,678 for the vehicle. That's $1,911 more in interest charges over the life of the loan.

	36 Months	60 Months
Final Purchase Price	$24,000	$24,000
10% Down Payment	$2,400	$2,400
Amount Financed	$21,600	$21,600
APR	12%	12%
Monthly Payment	$717.42	$480.48
Total Price (with interest)	$28,227	$31,228

Example #3. Three years and five years at 12 percent

Example #3 shows the effect of having a credit score below average. To qualify for a loan, you'd need to pay an APR of 12 percent. If you took on a three-year loan, your monthly payment would be $717.42—much higher than $676.86 if you qualified for 8 percent or $657.11 at 6 percent. If your credit score is poor, expect to be required to make a larger down payment.

Be sure to take advantage of free, online-based car loan calculators to help determine what financing options make sense for you. You can quickly calculate your monthly payment and the total price of the vehicle, based on the APR and loan term. You can also determine if leasing a car is a more viable financial option.

You can find a variety of auto-related finance calculators at these Web sites:

- **Yahoo! Autos**—*autos.yahoo.com/finance/loan-calc/index.html*
- **Vehix.com**—*www.vehix.com/finance/calculators/AutoLoan.aspx*
- **Cars.com**—*www.cars.com/go/advice/financing/calc/loanCalc.jsp*
- **Bankrate.com**—*www.bankrate.com/brm/rate/auto_home.asp*

SMART-DEBT STRATEGY

After analyzing the various car financing options, if you're a homeowner, you might find it smarter to pay for the vehicle by using a home equity loan or a home equity line of credit or even by refinancing your mortgage. You could qualify for a better interest rate and probably get tax advantages that don't exist with car loans. Explore all of your options fully. An accountant or financial planner can help you determine if these alterative financing options would be beneficial to you.

Completing a Loan Application

When applying for credit/financing through a dealership, you'll be required to provide personal and financial information that includes the following:

- Full name
- Current address and phone number (plus old addresses if you've moved within the past three years)
- A copy of your driver's license
- Social Security number
- Date of birth
- Three years of employment history
- Occupation
- Income
- Details about checking and savings accounts

You'll also need to give the dealer or lender permission to access your credit report(s) and credit score(s).

SMART-DEBT STRATEGY

When financing a vehicle, the purchase price and the terms of the financing should be two totally separate negotiations. First, negotiate the best price for the vehicle. Next, negotiate the value of your trade-in, if any. Finally, negotiate for the best financing. These should be separate negotiations, even though you may be dealing with the same person at the dealership. Don't allow the salesperson or dealership's financing manager to offer you a deal based on whatever monthly payment you say you're looking to make and can afford.

The financing deal offered by your dealer will often be at a higher rate than you'd qualify to receive from a bank or a credit union. Your dealer will typically not tell you that you could qualify for a better rate elsewhere. Remember: you are expected to negotiate!

Leasing a Vehicle

Some people choose to lease instead of purchasing. A lease is for a specified period of time. When the lease runs out, you return the vehicle to the dealership. You never actually own the vehicle. The benefit to a lease is that the monthly payment on the lease is typically lower than if you were to purchase the vehicle. The drawback is that you don't own the vehicle. At the end of the lease (typically between two and four years), you return the car and must then lease or purchase another vehicle. In some situations, you can negotiate to purchase the leased vehicle.

Before agreeing to a lease, it's important to determine your driving habits and expected usage of the vehicle. All leases set a limit on the number of miles you're allowed to drive per year—usually no more than 15,000 miles. Beyond that, in addition to the monthly payment, you'll be responsible for paying anywhere from 20 to 60 cents per mile. Another drawback to a lease is that if you want or need to get rid of the car early, you'll typically be charged a hefty early-termination fee. During the lease, you're also responsible for maintenance. At the end of the lease, you will be charged extra for excessive wear-and-tear on the vehicle, including any damage. Also, throughout the entire lease period, you must maintain an insurance policy that meets the leasing company's requirements.

SMART-DEBT STRATEGY

Contrary to popular belief, the monthly payment amount on a lease is often negotiable. The lease price is typically based on the sticker price of the vehicle, with no discounts taken into account. You should negotiate as if you're buying the car. In addition to the monthly lease payment, you can also negotiate the annual mileage limit and the purchase-option price (the price you would pay to purchase the vehicle after the lease expires). All negotiations should be done after you decide exactly what options and accessories you want added to the car.

Remember: in addition to the monthly lease payment, you'll be responsible for paying for insurance, gas, maintenance, and registration and inspection. When leasing a vehicle, instead of making a down payment, you will often need to pay your first month's lease payment, a refundable security deposit, and other fees (license, registration, title, etc.). There may also be an *acquisition fee* (also called a *processing* or *assignment fee*), freight/destination charges, as well as local and/or state taxes.

SMART-DEBT STRATEGY

To learn more about the pros and cons of leasing a vehicle, visit the Federal Reserve Board Web site, *www.federalreserve.gov/pubs/leasing*.

SMART-DEBT STRATEGY

Once you take on any type of car payment, whether for a loan or a lease, if you're late making payments or you skip payments, this negative information will be reported to the credit bureaus and it will negatively impact your credit score. Just as it's vital that you make your mortgage and credit card payments on time, the same is true for your car payments.

Other Car Considerations

A lot of factors go into buying or leasing a car. This chapter has provided guidance for dealing with some of the financial considerations. It's an excellent idea to pick up a few car buying guides that go beyond just the financial decisions you'll need to make.

For many people, buying or leasing a car is an unpleasant and stressful experience. Not only are some dealers and salespeople unethical in their sales practices, but the process itself can be confusing even if you totally trust the dealer and/or salesperson. Your best bet when shopping for a car is to do research before talking with dealers, taking test drives, and shopping around. Know what you're looking for and know what you can afford. Once you find a make and model vehicle you really like, it's totally acceptable to shop at two or even three dealerships for that vehicle.

Before ever stepping foot in a car dealership, consider using the Internet as a powerful research tool. Learn as much as you can about the type of car you're interested in and what your finance options are based on your financial situation and credit score. The more you learn in advance, the easier it will be to negotiate your best deal with the dealer or private seller and the lender. In almost every situation, you are expected to negotiate the best price and financing. Don't settle for the sticker price or suggested retail price of the vehicle and don't automatically accept the first financing deal you're offered, whether it's from the dealership, a bank, a credit union, or any other type of financial institution.

It's important to make all of the right decisions before signing the purchase or lease contracts. (This is especially true when buying a new car. The moment you drive it off the dealer's lot, your car drops in value immediately, as it goes from new to used.) By applying the smart debt-principles you've been learning, your car decisions should make good economic sense for your financial situation.

Don't take on more debt than absolutely necessary. Consider practicality and the smart-debt principles, rather than focusing on the vehicle as a status symbol. Financially, it might make a lot more sense for you to drive a new Honda Accord, for example, than a higher-priced BWM or Mercedes. Also, while you want to make sure you can afford the monthly payment, calculate and consider the overall price of the vehicle.

*   *   *

The next chapter of *Smart Debt* deals with the proper management of credit cards and credit card-related debt.

CHAPTER 6 | Credit Card Smart Debt Strategies

S tatistics released by the Federal Reserve Board indicate that more than 40 percent of American families are spending more than they earn. The most popular way of doing this is through the misuse or abuse of credit cards. While a credit card can be used occasionally in a short-term cash shortage and as a convenience when making purchases, improper use of credit cards costs consumers a lot of money in fees and interest charges and increases debt.

For example, if you have a credit card with an interest rate of 18 percent and you run up a balance of $8,000, if you pay only the monthly minimum, it will take you more than 25 years to completely pay off that debt—and cost you more than $24,000. Talk about wasting money! To see how long it'll take you to pay off your current credit card balances if you make only minimum payments, use the free online calculator at CardWeb.com (*www.cardweb.com/cardtrak/calc/payment.amp*).

If you use credit cards to cover your regular living expenses because you're spending more than you earn, eventually you will reach the credit limits on all of your cards and max them all out. At this point, you will not only be unable to pay your monthly living expenses, but also be unable to make the monthly payments on those high balances. This will put you deeper into debt, damage your credit score, and possibly lead to financial disaster.

Contrary to popular belief, even though a credit card is considered an unsecured loan, if you stop paying your monthly minimums, the creditor closes your account and charges it off, but the credit card issuer can legally come after you for the money you owe and often will do so.

At first, you'll receive an obscene number of collection calls and letters from your creditor. If you still don't pay, your account will eventually be sent to a collection agency. At this point, your credit score will take a huge dip, negative information will be placed on your credit report (where it will stay for seven years), and the collection agency will most likely take legal action. If you own a home, the judge may allow a lien to be placed on it. The judge may allow the creditor or collection agency to garnishee your future wages. In other words, it's not possible to simply walk away from credit card debt unless you declare bankruptcy. And that has become extremely difficult.

In addition to getting into legal trouble, if you default on credit card debt obligations, it will destroy your credit rating and credit score, which will prevent you from obtaining any loans or credit for many years. You will be unable, for example, to take out a mortgage, finance a car, or obtain a student loan.

The credit card companies are making profits of billions of dollars each year thanks to consumers who manage their credit cards badly and do not apply basic smart-debt principles in using them. There's no reason whatsoever why you can't use credit cards, but you always want to follow smart-debt principles to save money and protect your credit rating.

What to Consider *Before* Using a Credit Card

This chapter is all about credit cards and smart-debt principles you should immediately begin applying to your credit cards. If you're going to own and use credit cards successfully, you'll need to consider your actions from three perspectives.

First, consider the financial consequences of using those credit cards and the long-term cost. This means finding the best credit card deals, shopping around for the best rates, focusing on APRs and fees, and then being wise about using your cards.

Second, focus on the impact of your credit cards on your credit score and your credit reports. The number of active accounts you have, the balances you maintain, and your record of monthly payments all get reported to the credit bureaus—Equifax, Experian, and TransUnion. These bureaus then incorporate this information into your credit reports. Those credit reports, as we've discussed, generate your credit scores. (See Chapter 2 for information about the credit bureaus, your credit report, and your credit score.) Even one late credit card payment could cause your credit score to drop. If an account goes to collections or gets charged off by the creditor, this will negatively impact your credit score for seven years.

Finally, focus on applying smart-debt principles to your credit cards. This means acquiring only the credit you need, only when you need it, maintaining balances you can afford, shopping around for the best deals, and having a plan to pay off balances in a relatively short time to minimize interest and fees on insignificant purchases. As you'll discover from this chapter, using your credit cards for insignificant purchases, such as dining out, movie tickets, dry cleaning bills, etc., and then taking months or years to pay off that debt is simply throwing away money. It's a classic example of bad debt, definitely not smart debt.

If you're going to use a credit card to make insignificant purchases for convenience or to use the credit card's reward system, that's fine, as long as you have a plan to pay off the balance at the end of the month, especially if the card has a high interest rate. There are situations, however, when it might make sense to carry a balance on a credit card, especially if you're offered an introductory or promotional zero interest rate for a few months, for example. Taking advantage of these special offers often makes sense, as long as you read all of the fine print and adhere to the terms of the offer.

What Are Credit Cards?

Credit cards—whether *bank cards* (like MasterCard, Visa, and Discover), *travel and entertainment cards* (such as many of the American Express products and Diners Club), or *house cards* (issued by retail store chains, department stores, gas stations, and other companies that cater to consumers)—are a form of revolving credit. That means that you can carry an account balance from one billing cycle to the next and you pay interest on that balance. Your balance cannot exceed the specified credit limit and you must pay at least the specified minimum every month, typically between two and two-and-a-half percent of the balance.

Buying anything using a credit card is just like taking out a loan. Credit cards are *not* free money or a license to spend money until you reach your credit limit and max out the card! They're cost-effective and worthwhile only if we use them responsibly.

Every credit card issuer sets terms to which a cardholder (borrower) must adhere to in order to keep his or her account active and in good standing. These terms are described in the cardholders' agreement that's provided to everyone who opens an account. In addition to all of the rules and regulations, the agreement states the card's annual percentage rate (APR)—the cost of credit expressed as a yearly rate. This number, along with the periodic rate (the cost of credit for the billing period), will help you calculate how much maintaining a balance on the credit card will cost you over time.

CHARGE CARDS AND DEBIT CARDS

The term *credit card* and *charge card* are often used interchangeably. However, they are not the same. Purchases made with a *credit card* can be paid off over time: it's revolving credit. With a *charge card* the cardholder must pay off the balance in full each month when the statement arrives. (While American Express is known for its credit cards, some of its products are actually charge cards.)

A *debit card* is also very different from a credit card or a charge card. While a debit card may display the Visa or MasterCard logo, meaning that it can be used to make purchases from companies that accept Visa or MasterCard, when you make a purchase using a debit card, the amount of that purchase is automatically withdrawn from your checking or savings account within a few days. A debit card is a more convenient alternative to writing a check or paying with cash; there is no credit.

THE BENEFITS AND DRAWBACKS OF CREDIT CARDS

The following is a list of potential benefits of using a major credit card:

- You can buy items you need right away; you don't need to save up for them—"buy now, pay later," as opposed to "buy now, pay now" using cash, a check, or a debit card. A credit card provides an unsecured loan, entailing interest and finance charges (if you don't pay in full) and fees.
- You don't need to carry around a lot of cash.
- Your monthly statement provides a detailed record of your purchases.

- Using a credit card is faster and much more convenient than writing checks.
- If managed properly, you can consolidate multiple bills into one payment.
- Using a credit card is typically more secure than using cash or checks.
- Certain credit cards offer perks, such as cash-back rewards and frequent flier miles.
- If you shop around for the best credit card deals and manage your accounts wisely, you can get low interest rates, special introductory offers, balance transfer offers, and other cost-saving benefits.

Credit cards also have some potential drawbacks, especially for people who don't manage them wisely. Here are some that can be costly:

- You'll pay extra for purchase using credit cards, thanks to interest, fees, and finance charges, especially if you pay the balances over time.
- The convenience of credit cards makes it extremely easy to spend beyond your means, which will result in financial difficulties and large amounts of debt.
- You can negatively impact your credit record and credit score if you don't pay your credit card bills on time every month. This will ultimately make it more difficult and much more expensive to get a car loan, a mortgage, or even insurance.

TYPES OF CREDIT CARDS

Not all credit cards are alike. There are differences in interest rates and fees, of course. Cards also differ in their purposes and the ways in which they are promoted. Some cards are intended for people with problematic credit records, for example, while other cards offer rebates, bonuses, or other incentives for using them. These are the types of cards available.

- **Traditional/General-Use Credit Card**—This is a traditional, revolving-credit card, such as Visa, MasterCard, Discover, and some American Express cards. These cards are issued by banks, credit unions, and other financial institutions.
- **Affinity Credit Card**—This is a traditional credit card with a twist. An affinity card is a Visa or a MasterCard affiliated with an organization, branded to show that affiliation, and entitling cardholders to spe-

cial discounts or deals from the organization. Major retailers—such as Barnes & Noble Booksellers, Sony, Wal-Mart, Starbucks, Jet Blue Airlines, American Airlines, The Walt Disney Company, and thousands more—and hundreds of charitable organizations and colleges and universities offer affinity credit cards. Most affinity credit cards have an annual fee and a slightly higher interest rate, but the incentives or perks can be worth the extra costs. It's been estimated that about a third of the credit cards in use now are affinity cards. JPMorgan Chase & Company (*www.chase.com/PFSCreditCardHome.html*), for example, offers over 180 affinity MasterCard and Visa credit cards, and MBNA Corporation (*www.mbna.com/creditcards/directory.html*) offers a similar number.

- **Premium Credit Card**—This a credit card that offers incentives, such as cash-back rebates on purchases, frequent flier miles, insurance, etc. Premium credit cards offer high credit limits and are usually available only to people with excellent credit. An affinity card can also be a premium credit card.
- **Debit Card**—This is a card that transfers payments directly from the cardholder's bank account. Some cards require a personal identification number (PIN). Others require the cardholder's signature. A PIN-based or direct debit card makes transfers almost immediately; a signature-based or deferred debit card has a Visa or MasterCard logo and makes transfers in two or three days.
- **Prepaid/Gift Card**—This type of card displays the Visa or MasterCard logo and is accepted wherever major credit cards are accepted. However, these are not credit cards; they are basically gift certificates. You simply pay $X for a card and you can make $X in purchases. There's no need to open an account with a creditor and card usage is not reported to the credit bureaus and does not impact your credit report or credit score.
- **Secured Credit Card**—This type of card works just like any other major credit card (Visa or MasterCard), but it draws upon a special account managed by the card issuer that consists of money deposited in advance by the cardholder. Most credit cards are "buy now, pay later"; secured credit cards are "pay now, buy later." The account secures all purchases up to the limit, the amount on deposit. These cards are much like prepaid/gift cards, but with a variety of fees and a big benefit. The benefit is that the accounts are reported to the credit-

reporting agencies as regular credit cards, so secured cards offer a way for people with credit problems to begin establishing or rebuilding credit by showing their ability to manage their card accounts.

SMART-DEBT STRATEGY

Understanding how credit cards work can be confusing. After reading this chapter, if you have unanswered questions, the Federal Trade Commission offers a free, comprehensive 24-page guide, *Getting Credit: What You Need to Know About Your Credit.* You can download it at *www.ftc.gov/gettingcredit.*

Credit Card Statistics

As of April 2005, credit card debt in the United States totaled over $735 billion. This debt was generated by the 185 million American consumers who currently have at least one credit card. The average credit card debt per household is over $8,400. More than 20 percent of credit card holders have maxed out their cards.

Using Credit Cards According to Smart-Debt Principles

Of all the ways consumers can borrow money and acquire debt, credit cards tend to be the most troublesome. Most consumers don't fully understand how credit cards work and the financial implications of using them. Even fewer take the time to shop around for the best deals, properly manage their accounts, and use smart-debt principles to save money and preserve their credit rating and credit score.

Because most credit card purchases are paid for over time, interest and fees add to the cost, so the average purchase made on a credit card winds up costing the cardholder considerably more than if he or she had used cash. According to CardWeb.com, "On average, the typical credit card purchase is 112 percent higher than if using cash."

Since most consumers don't shop around for the best credit card deals, they wind up paying extremely high interest rates and fees. In fact, Americans pay an average of 18.9 percent interest on each of their credit cards. Simply by shopping around for better credit card deals, you can save a fortune every year.

The following are some of the basic smart-debt principles you should apply to your credit card:

- Apply for credit cards that have the lowest interest rates and fees. Read the fine print of the cardholders' agreement carefully to make sure you understand all of the fees associated with the card. There may be an annual fee, account maintenance charges, over-the-limit charges, late fees, cash advance fees, ATM fees, and other charges that will add up quickly.

- Don't use credit cards for everyday purchases unless you have a plan and the funds to pay off the balance at the end of the month, to avoid incurring interest charges.

- To maintain the highest possible credit score, always pay at least the minimum monthly payment on time for each credit card.

- To maintain the highest possible credit score, keep your credit card balances below 35 percent of each card's limit. Instead of maintaining a high balance on one or two cards, try to maintain lower balances on several cards at competitive interest rates.

- Always try to pay more than your minimum monthly payments. When you make purchases using a credit card, plan for paying off the debt quickly.

- Don't use your credit cards for cash advances, especially if the interest rate and fees for this convenience are high.

- If you already have high balances on several high-interest credit cards, consider applying for lower-interest credit cards with attractive balance transfer offers and take advantage of the no-interest or low-interest offers to save money. (Credit card balance transfers are described later in this chapter.) Ultimately, you want to maintain a zero balance on your high-interest credit cards. But don't close those accounts if you've had them open for several years. When calculating your credit scores, the credit bureaus review how long you've had credit card accounts open and in good standing.

- Never apply for multiple credit cards in a short period of time. Each card issuer will check your credit; if the inquiries exceed the norm, it will negatively impact your credit report. Try to spread out your credit card applications by at least six months.

- As a general rule, store-issued credit cards or charge cards typically have higher fees and interest rates than traditional credit cards. Even if the initial offer for a house card seems attractive, read the fine print carefully. In most cases, you're better off using one of your regular, low-interest credit cards for those big-ticket items. If you don't absolutely need an additional credit card to make a purchase, don't apply for it, no matter how many times the salesperson tells you how much money you could save.

CREDIT CARD LINGO YOU SHOULD UNDERSTAND

Responsibly managing your credit card accounts involves understanding the terms and conditions imposed by the credit card issuer. Be sure to read the cardholders' agreement carefully for each of your accounts.

To help you better understand credit card offers when shopping for the best deals, here are some essential terms:

- **Annual fee**—This is a fee you pay every year for the privilege of having a specific credit card. Depending on the card, the annual fee might range from zero to $150. Ideally, you want a credit card with no annual fee. If the card offers some reward for usage (such as airline miles) or a cash-back bonus, an annual fee will often apply.
- **Annual percentage rate (APR)**—This is a measure of the cost of credit, the amount of interest you'll pay per year on your balance for that card. The APR could be different if you use the card for cash advances or transfer a balance from another card.
- **Average daily balance**—This is the method the credit card issuer uses to calculate your payment due. Your average daily balance is calculated by adding each day's balance and then dividing that total by the number of days in a billing cycle. Your average daily balance is then multiplied by the card's monthly periodic rate, which is calculated by dividing the APR by 12.
- **Balance transfer and balance transfer rate**—A balance transfer involves moving a balance from one credit card to another, generally one with a lower interest rate, in order to save money on interest charges. In order to entice consumers to transfer their debt (and whatever interest and fees it will generate in the future), many credit card issuers offer special incentive or teaser rates on balance transfers. The balance transfer rate is the APR you'll be paying on the balance you transfer to the new card. If you're being offered a special teaser rate, find out what the APR will be when that teaser rate expires. Read the cardholders' agreement carefully. Be aware that transfers

may involve additional fees, so understand the terms and conditions on both credit cards.

- **Cardholders' agreement**—This is the "fine print" associated with each credit card. It lists all of the terms and conditions, fees, and other information a card holder should know about using that card.
- **Cash advance fee**—Many credit cards are accompanied by a PIN (personal identification number) that allows you to use that card to withdraw money from an ATM—cash advances. Depending on the credit card issuer, you might be charged a flat fee for each ATM transaction or a fee that's a percentage of the amount withdrawn (and possibly a flat fee as well). Often, the portion of your credit card balance that's a total of cash advances will be charged a higher APR. Read the cardholders' agreement carefully.
- **Charge off**—This is an action that a creditor takes when it is not expected that a credit card balance will be paid: it writes it off as a bad debt. The debt is then marked on the cardholder's credit reports as charged off. This is a big negative. When a balance is charged off, the account is automatically closed, but the debt still exists and attempts will be made to collect it.
- **Grace period**— Time during which a lender charges no interest on credit card purchases. If a cardholder has a zero balance on his or her credit card and uses the card to make purchases, the grace period is the time between the day of the purchases and the day on which finance charges (interest, etc.) will start for the new balance. If no grace period is offered, finance charges will accrue from the moment a purchase is made. If the cardholder already has a balance on his or her credit card, a grace period does not apply. A grace period is typically between 20 and 30 days.
- **Minimum payment**—This is the lowest amount a cardholder must pay to keep his or her credit card account from going into default and to avoid a negative report to the credit bureaus. The minimum payment is typically about two percent of the balance. Remember: simply making the minimum payment each month will do very little to lower your balance. This strategy will ultimately cost you more in interest charges. For your specific credit cards, use the Minimum Payment Calculator on the BankRate.com Web site (*www.bankrate. com/brm/calc/MinPayment.asp*) to see how much maintaining a bal-

ance is costing you over time. For example, if you currently have a balance of $1,000 on a credit card that charges 18 percent interest and you pay just the monthly minimum of 2 percent ($20.00), it will take you 232 months (over 19 years) to be rid of your debt. In that time, you will pay $1,931.33 in interest.

- **Over-the-limit fee**—If your charges and fees combined go over your card's credit limit in any given billing cycle, you will be charged this additional fee. Many credit card issuers charge an over-the-limit fee of $35.
- **Transaction fees and other charges**—These are extra fees you'll pay to use your credit card for certain types of transactions, such as ATM (cash advance) withdrawals, making a payment late, or going over your credit limit.

SMART-DEBT STRATEGY

For each credit card you have, become familiar with the terms and fees set forth in the cardholders' agreement. Every credit card account will come with a different agreement and have different fees and rates. Don't just read one cardholders' agreement and assume that the agreements for your other cards are the same, even for cards from the same bank, financial institution, or card issuer.

ALWAYS SHOP AROUND FOR THE BEST CREDIT CARD DEALS

Choosing the best credit card offer(s) to apply for requires careful shopping and comparisons between offers, especially if your credit score is average or below average. While many credit card issuers (such as Capital One, First Premier, Orchard Bank, and New Millennium Bank) will approve a credit card application from someone with a low credit score, the APR and fees for those credit cards will often be astronomical and the credit limit will be very low.

For example, one credit card offer that targeted people with below-average credit scores offered a 19.75 percent APR with a 25.75 percent cash advance APR, a 25.75 percent delinquency APR for purchases, and a 31.75 percent delinquency APR for cash advances. In addition, this particular card has a $150.00 annual fee, a $29.00 one-time account opening fee, and a $6.50 monthly account maintenance fee. Additional fees associated with this card included a transaction fee of 5 percent for cash advances, a $35.00 late payment fee (in addition to the higher APR), and a $35.00

over-the-limit fee. According to the credit card issuer, "The delinquency APR will apply in the event that you do not pay the required minimum payment by its due date for two consecutive billing cycles or for any four billing cycles in any 12-month period." This offer is a far cry from those credit cards with 0 percent interest rates for one year and no annual fee that companies offer to consumers with excellent credit.

If someone with a low credit score and a poor credit history wants to reestablish credit and begin rebuilding his or her credit score, it is often necessary to take advantage of less attractive credit card offers for a few years. Anyone who pursues this option, however, should make sure he or she is able to use the credit card carefully to stay current and avoid any excess charges (late fees, etc.).

In addition to contacting your local bank, credit union, or other financial institution, to compare credit cards or secured credit cards, visit any of these sites:

- moneycentral.msn.com/banking/services/creditcard.asp
- www.bankrate.com
- www.cardratings.com
- www.cardweb.com
- www.chase.com/PFSCreditCardHome.html
- www.creditcards.com
- www.creditcardscenter.com
- www.e-wisdom.com/credit_cards/chart.html
- www.lowermybills.com

SMART-DEBT STRATEGY

College students trying to establish credit can take advantage of a variety of special credit card offers. Proof of being a full-time student is required to take advantage of these offers. Credit card offers targeted specifically to college students are advertised on college campuses and are often mailed directly to college students. Remember: managing these credit card accounts improperly could destroy your credit rating and reduce your credit score.

Managing Your Credit Card Accounts

Now you've hopefully taken the first step toward applying the smart-debt principles to credit card management and you have successfully shopped around for the very best credit card deals available for your credit situation and needs. The rest of this chapter focuses on specific strategies for using your credit cards.

Use the Expanded Credit Card Management Worksheet below to better manage your credit card accounts.

Expanded Credit Card Management Worksheet

Using the information from Worksheets #7 and #8 in Chapter 1, as well as your most recent credit card statements and the cardholders' agreement, use this worksheet to help manage your credit card debt, decide whether or not to consolidate your balances, and track the cost of maintaining the debt over time. Fill out the form for each of your credit card accounts.

Credit Card #1 Account Information

Credit Card Name	
Account Number	
Interest Rate (APR)	
Credit Card Issuer's Phone Number	
Credit Card Issuer's Web Site Address (Username and Password)	
Credit Limit	$
Target Balance (35% of the Credit Limit)	$
Current Balance as of ___ / ___ / ___	$
Monthly Minimum Payment	$
Actual Monthly Payment Made	$
Monthly Interest Paid	$

Credit Card #2 Account Information

Credit Card Name	
Account Number	
Interest Rate (APR)	
Credit Card Issuer's Phone Number	
Credit Card Issuer's Web Site Address (Username and Password)	
Credit Limit	$
Target Balance (35% of the Credit Limit)	$
Current Balance as of ___ / ___ / ___	$
Monthly Minimum Payment	$
Actual Monthly Payment Made	$
Monthly Interest Paid	$

Credit Card #3 Account Information

Credit Card Name	
Account Number	
Interest Rate (APR)	
Credit Card Issuer's Phone Number	
Credit Card Issuer's Web Site Address (Username and Password)	
Credit Limit	$
Target Balance (35% of the Credit Limit)	$
Current Balance as of ___ / ___ / ___	$
Monthly Minimum Payment	$
Actual Monthly Payment Made	$
Monthly Interest Paid	$

Credit Card Smart Debt Strategies

Credit Card #4 Account Information

Credit Card Name	
Account Number	
Interest Rate (APR)	
Credit Card Issuer's Phone Number	
Credit Card Issuer's Web Site Address (Username and Password)	
Credit Limit	$
Target Balance (35% of the Credit Limit)	$
Current Balance as of ___ / ___ / ___	$
Monthly Minimum Payment	$
Actual Monthly Payment Made	$
Monthly Interest Paid	$

Credit Card #5 Account Information

Credit Card Name	
Account Number	
Interest Rate (APR)	
Credit Card Issuer's Phone Number	
Credit Card Issuer's Web Site Address (Username and Password)	
Credit Limit	$
Target Balance (35% of the Credit Limit)	$
Current Balance as of ___ / ___ / ___	$
Monthly Minimum Payment	$
Actual Monthly Payment Made	$
Monthly Interest Paid	$

Credit Card Debt Summary Worksheet

Total Credit Card Debt	$
Total Monthly Minimum Payment (All Credit Card Accounts)	$
Total Actual Monthly Payment (All Credit Card Accounts)	$
Total Monthly Interest Paid	$
Percentage of Total Credit Actually Being Used (100% would mean all of your credit cards are maxed out.)	

SMART-DEBT STRATEGY

As you're reviewing each of your credit card accounts, determine if you have any cards with a high interest rate and a high balance. Could you benefit from opening another credit card account (one with no annual fee, a low interest rate, and an attractive balance transfer offer) and transferring your balance to that card? See the section below on credit card balance transfers for details on how to do this effectively to save money.

USEFUL ONLINE CALCULATORS

The following free online calculators will help you better manage your credit card debt:

Debt Consolidation Calculator, *www.debtcalculator-online.com/debt_consolidation_calculator.htm*. Use this calculator to figure out whether or not it makes sense to consolidate your credit card balances.

Debt Pay-Off Calculator, *www.debtcalculator-online.com/debt_payoff_calculator%20.htm* or *www.bankrate.com/brm/calc/MinPayment.asp*. This calculator will help you compute how much you will need to pay each month in order to pay off a given debt by a goal date that you select.

Credit Card Interest Payment Calculator, *www.bankrate.com/brm/calc/MinPayment.asp*. This calculator will show how much interest you will be paying if you make only the minimum required payment. It will also tell you how many minimum payments it will take to pay off your balance.

Two More Strategies for Managing Your Credit Cards

Chapter 2 presented ten strategies for improving a bad credit situation. Those strategies are not just for people in financial trouble; you can also use them, starting immediately, to more effectively manage your credit card accounts, protect your credit rating, and save money. Remember: from month to month, your goal should always be to pay down or pay off your credit card balances, not allow them to increase. Now we'll consider two more strategies.

TAKE ADVANTAGE OF SPECIAL BALANCE TRANSFER OFFERS

One of the ways credit card companies entice consumers to apply for their cards is to offer extremely attractive balance transfer offers. They can be an effective strategy for managing your credit card debt—if you're smart in using them.

Suppose you currently have a credit card with an 18 percent interest rate and a $6,000 balance. Your minimum payment would be $150, of which $90 would go toward interest charges. If you don't add any new charges to the account, but pay only the minimum each month, it would take 331 months (more than 27 years) to pay off the debt. Ultimately, you'd pay $8,615.25 in interest on that $6,000 debt.

To reduce the interest and save money, you could seek out and apply for a new, low-interest credit card that offers an attractive balance transfer rate. You would move your $6,000 balance to the new credit card and take on the terms associated with the new credit card while paying off the balance of the old card.

If you shop around and your credit score is average or better, you can often find very attractive new credit card offers that allow for a no-cost balance transfer with zero percent interest for the first six months to one year, for example. After that, normal interest charges apply. The benefit to transferring your high-interest balance to a zero-interest credit card, even if it's only for six months to one year, can be significant. On that $6,000 balance in our example, you could save up to $90 per month in interest charges, even if you make only the minimum monthly payments.

When the period of zero-percent interest expires, you could continue making your regular monthly payments. If that new credit card has a lower interest rate (after the special offer expires) than your old card, you'll continue to save money. If not or if you find another credit card offering an attractive balance transfer offer, you can move your balance again.

SMART-DEBT STRATEGY

To pay off your credit card debt even faster, one strategy is to transfer your balance to a card with zero-interest introductory rate, but keep making the same minimum payments as on the old card (at least two percent of the balance). Instead of spending your new-found savings, apply them to paying off your debt faster.

The first step in transferring a balance is to analyze which of your account balances it would make the most sense to transfer to lower-interest accounts. Take a look at the Expanded Credit Card Management Worksheet you completed earlier in this chapter. Select the accounts with the highest balances and the highest interest rates.

Next, shop around for new credit card offers that feature a zero-percent or extremely low interest rate for balance transfers. When you find one that looks best, carefully read the cardholders' agreement to ensure you understand all of the terms, the length of the period for introductory interest rate, and the interest rate when the introductory period expires.

SMART-DEBT STRATEGY

Depending on the credit card issuer, the special offer for an introductory balance transfer rate and the fees for transferring a balance may be very different from the "introductory APR" offered for new purchases made with the card. Make sure you know the APR, fees, and expiration dates for balance transfers and that you have this information in writing.

When you've decided on a new credit card, fill out the application. Be sure to make it clear that you intend to take advantage of the balance transfer offer. You will need to provide details about your current credit card and the balance you wish to transfer. The approval process could take several weeks. Continue to make the minimum monthly payments on your current credit card account until you receive written notice that you now have the new card, that the balance has been transferred, and that your old card now has a zero balance. You may want to call the old credit card company to confirm the transfer.

SMART-DEBT STRATEGY

In many cases, an attractive balance transfer offer applies only to new accounts. The balance transfer must be initiated at the time the credit card application is completed. Otherwise, the introductory balance transfer rate will not apply once the new account is opened and the card is issued. Read the Terms and Conditions of the credit card offer in addition to the cardholders' agreement.

Record the date of the balance transfer and calculate when the special introductory offer will expire. You may want to take additional actions as you get closer to the expiration date, before interest charges start accumulating on the outstanding balance.

The CreditCards.com Web site (*www.creditcards.com*) allows you to quickly shop around for credit cards offering attractive balance transfer rates to new cardholders. As you search for the best offers, look for statements like "0% interest for up to 12 months on all purchases and balance transfers," "0% APR on balance transfers for 12 months," "This credit card features a low 0% introductory APR on balance transfers for up to 6 months," or "0.00% intro rate for 6 months on purchases and balance transfers."

SHOULD YOU CONSIDER DEBT CONSOLIDATION?

Taking advantage of special balance transfer offers is a "quick fix" to stop paying high interest rates on a small number of high-interest credit card accounts. However, if you're already in serious debt and have many high-interest credit cards that are maxed out or close to it, you should consider a debt consolidation loan as a more viable long-term fix to your situation.

A debt consolidation loan could allow you to take several high-interest credit card accounts and combine them into a loan at a lower interest rate. If you have three, four, or more credit cards with high balances at 10 percent, 15 percent, or even 20 percent, you could combine all of those balances into one loan with an interest rate of less than eight percent, for example, if you have a decent credit score.

Not only will you immediately begin saving money each month in interest charges, you'll also zero out your credit card balances and have only one payment to make each month. The trick is to either close your credit card accounts once they're paid off or have the discipline to stop using them altogether.

Debt consolidation loans are typically offered to homeowners. You can refinance your current mortgage, apply for a second mortgage, or use a home equity loan or a home equity line of credit to pay off your credit card debt and consolidate the balances. The potential drawback to this is that you're transferring your debt from unsecured credit to a secured loan, with your home as collateral. Thus, if you default on your loan, you could ultimately lose your house.

If, however, you're able to make the monthly payments on your debt consolidation loan, you will save significant money and be able to protect your credit rating. It's important to take this step early on, however—before you get so far behind with your credit card payments that your credit score takes a huge hit.

A debt consolidation loan doesn't eliminate the debt. It simply allows you to take high-interest credit card debts, combine them into one lower-interest loan, and then pay off that loan over time while saving money each month on interest charges.

Be sure to read Chapters 3 and 4 for more information about refinancing your mortgage or taking out a second mortgage as a way of consolidating your debt. Make sure the fees, closing costs, and interest charges associated with the new loan allow you to achieve your financial objectives and you're not simply trading one high-interest loan for another kind of high-interest loan.

An accountant, financial planner, or credit counselor will be able to help you determine if a debt consolidation loan is worthwhile, based on your current financial situation, amount of debt, and credit rating.

What to Do if Your Credit Cards Get Lost or Stolen

Let's face it: people sometimes lose their wallet or purse, misplace a credit card, or become victims of theft. Having your credit card, debit card, or ATM card information fall into the wrong hands is one of the biggest causes of identity theft, which can ultimate cost you a fortune. If any of your credit cards get lost or stolen or you believe your confidential account information is in any way compromised, call the credit card issuers immediately to report the problem and have them suspend the accounts and issue you new cards.

Credit Card Smart Debt Strategies

At the same time, if your cards and/or your confidential account information are stolen, contact the police department and fill out a crime report and contact all three of the credit bureaus. Then, for the next six to 12 months, watch your credit card statements and your credit report carefully. Look for any unauthorized charges or new accounts being opened in your name that you haven't authorized.

If any of your credit cards get lost or stolen, time is of the essence in reporting the loss or theft to the credit card issuers. The phone numbers to call should appear on your monthly statements. It's a good idea to keep all of the information from the Expanded Credit Card Management Worksheet (which you completed earlier in this chapter) in a secure place at home so you will have this information handy if you need to contact a credit card issuer.

In addition to calling the bank or financial institution that issued the credit card, you can also report a lost or stolen card to Visa, MasterCard, Discover, or American Express directly, using the following phone numbers that are available 24/7:

- Visa Global Customer Assistance Center: (800) 847-2911
- MasterCard Assistance Center: (800) 622-7747
- Discover: (800) DISCOVER (347-2683)
- American Express Emergency Card Replacement: (800) 528-2122

SMART-DEBT STRATEGY

After reporting your credit card(s) lost or stolen, follow up with a letter in writing to each credit card issuer, bank, or other financial institution. Within the letter, give your full name and address, account number, and details about the theft or loss (including the time and date).

While dealing with missing credit cards can be a hassle, the good news is that, under federal law, you're liable for unauthorized charges only up to $50 per card, assuming you report the loss or theft in a timely manner. Also, some homeowner's insurance policies cover lost or stolen credit cards.

One strategy for limiting your liability is to only carry one or two credit cards with you at any time. Keep the rest of your cards at home in a secure location. Most people have no need to carry more than their ATM card, one credit card, and some cash. Make a detailed inventory of financial and legal items that you ever carry in your wallet or purse, which would include information about all of your credit cards, ATM cards, debit cards, membership cards, driver's license, insurance cards, etc. Keep this inventory at home. This way, if your wallet or purse gets lost or stolen, you will know the numbers to call and have all of your account or membership numbers handy.

Remember: a person doesn't need to have your credit card in hand in order to make unauthorized charges. Keep your credit card number, expiration date, PIN, and the three-digit security number on the back of the card as private as possible. If you throw away old credit cards or statements, shred them so the numbers and confidential information are no longer legible. Also, never carry the PIN for your debit or credit card in your wallet or purse. This is a number you should memorize.

Protecting Yourself from Identity Theft

Identity theft is the unauthorized use of personal identification information to commit fraud or other crimes. One example would be if someone stole or found your credit card and used it to make purchases or used your identity to take out loans or establish credit in your name.

Discovering you've become a victim of identity theft or some other type of credit fraud can be extremely stressful and the experience can be costly if you do not handle it promptly and correctly. While you may be protected financially if you're a fraud victim, correcting the problem will still often require a lot of time and effort on your part.

Before you think to yourself, "Oh, that could never happen to me," consider these disturbing statistics offered by the Federal Trade Commission:

- In 2003, there were over 9,910,000 victims of identity theft in the United States.
- In 2004, identity theft resulted in $47,600,000,000 in losses in the United States.
- A victim of identity theft will have to spend 175 to 600 hours or more to restore his or her good name and recover from the ID theft.
- Someone falls victim to identity theft in the United States every four seconds.

The best way to prevent identity theft is to subscribe to a credit-monitoring service so you will be notified within 24 hours every time any type of change is made to your credit report. Thus, if someone uses your identity to apply for a credit card or some type of loan, for example, you will find out about it and can stop it before it's too late.

How can you know if you're a victim of identity theft? Here are several signs:

- Your credit reports will list new credit cards as having been issued in your name that you did not apply for or receive.
- Your credit reports will list information about accounts that you did not open and know nothing about.
- Your monthly credit card statements and/or bank statements will show charges that you did not authorize.
- You stop receiving monthly credit card statements and/or important bills.
- You start receiving bills from companies you've never done business with.
- You start receiving calls from creditors and/or collection agencies regarding accounts you know nothing about.

If you believe you've become a victim of identity theft or some type of credit-related fraud, here are some steps to follow:

- Contact your creditors and bank immediately to discuss your suspicions. If a credit card is lost or stolen or you notice potentially fraudulent charges on your statement, report that immediately to the bank or credit card issuer. The appropriate phone number will be listed on your statement.
- Contact your local police department immediately and file a report. Be sure to obtain a copy of this report.
- Collect all documents, such as your credit report, monthly statements, and other written information that relate to your suspicion. Keep detailed notes about the people with whom you speak and what notices you receive, etc. Do not destroy or throw away any related paperwork or files.
- If you believe someone is fraudulently using your Social Security number, contact the Federal Trade Commission at (877) IDTHEFT (438-4338). Under certain circumstances, the Social Security Administration may assign you a new SSN if you are still being "disadvantaged" by the misuse of your Social Security number after you have made all efforts to resolve the problems. Call (800) 772-1213.
- Change your password and PIN on all ATM, debit, and credit cards. Change your checking account number and related passwords and PINs as well.

- Contact the Fraud Victim Assistance department at each of the major credit-reporting agencies and ask that a "Fraud Alert" be placed in your credit report file. From this point forward, creditors will be instructed to take additional steps to verify your identity before granting credit in your name. Contact Equifax at (800) 525-6285, Experian at (888) 397-3742, and TransUnion at (800) 860-7289. Remember: the three credit-reporting agencies are not connected. Contacting just one of the three isn't enough. You must contact all three.

The Federal Trade Commission can be helpful if you're a victim of identity theft. Contact the ID Theft Clearinghouse at (877) ID-THEFT or visit this Web site: *www.consumer.gov/idtheft*. Once you report your identity theft or fraud suspicions, you may be required to complete an ID Theft Affidavit and/or a Fraudulent Account Statement. A group of credit grantors, consumer advocates, and the FTC developed these forms to help consumers report information to many companies using one standard form. This form can be obtained by calling the FTC's ID Theft Clearinghouse or visiting the organization's ID Theft Web site.

Learning to properly manage your credit card debt and take a responsible approach to obtaining and using credit cards is a skill, not just a set of concepts. Adopting a smart-debt strategy for your credit cards will save you a fortune over your lifetime.

* * *

The next chapter of *Smart Debt* focuses on utilizing smart-debt principles to pay for student loans.

CHAPTER 7 | Smart Debt 101 and Your Student Loans

Any type of postsecondary education is extremely expensive and the costs continue to climb with each passing semester—tuition, textbooks, supplies, dorm/housing fees, activities fees, a meal plan, health insurance, a computer.... This chapter is all about taking a smart-debt approach to managing student loans.

The chapter is divided into two main sections. The first part is for people who are paying off student loans. We'll explore options for transforming these existing loans into smart debt. The second part is geared to future students. It focuses on how to pay for postsecondary education in the future by taking a smart-debt approach to acquiring loans. This involves taking full advantage of scholarships, savings, equity in your home, government guaranteed loans, and private loans.

Unfortunately, paying for a postsecondary education has become not only extremely costly but also extremely complicated. By adopting a smart-debt approach to taking on new loans, you'll be able to pay for an education without paying extra fees, finance charges, and high interest for many years after graduation.

Repaying Student Loans

If you are in the process of paying off any student loans, take a few minutes to evaluate your situation and determine if you can adopt any smart-debt principles to lower your interest rate, reduce the time it'll take to pay off the loans, consolidate the loans to save money, or develop a more efficient plan for paying them off.

Refer back to Chapter 1 and, if you haven't already done so, complete Worksheet 1-6 (reproduced here as well).

Lender	Loan Description	Interest Rate (%)	Monthly Payment	Duration	Months/ Years Remaining
Total Monthly Payment			$		
Interest Paid This Month			$		

Evaluate each of your outstanding student loans and consider if any of the following smart-debt options make sense for you in your current financial situation:

- With your credit rating and credit score, could you refinance these loans with your current lender(s) to get a better rate and/or reduce the time it'll take to pay off the loans?
- Could you afford to make one or more extra payments toward the loan's principle each year in order to pay off the debt quicker and save money on interest? If so, start with the loans that have the highest interest rate.
- Are you a homeowner with equity in your home? Would it make financial sense to consolidate your student loans by refinancing your current mortgage, taking out a home equity loan, or using a home equity line of credit to pay off the student loans? This wouldn't eliminate the debt, but perhaps you could consolidate the loans into one lower-interest loan and benefit from the tax advantages of using your home.
- If you're experiencing serious financial trouble right now, should you contact your lenders and defer payments on the loans for a few months until you regain your financial stability?

Anything you can do to pay off student loans faster or reduce the interest and fees would be considered taking a smart-debt approach.

SMART-DEBT STRATEGY

Student loans are just like any other type of debt, like your mortgage or credit cards. The lenders regularly report information about your debt to the three credit bureaus. If you make your monthly payments late, skip payments, or default on your loan(s), this will have a strong negative impact on your credit rating and credit score. As you know, anytime your credit score drops, your chances of being approved for future credit, loans, or financing decrease. If you are still able to borrow money, it will be at a higher interest rate, which ultimately costs you more.

If you run into financial problems, negotiate with your lenders. Don't ignore these loans or default on them. Negative information placed on your credit report remains there for up to seven years. Plus, defaulting on your own student loans could hamper your ability to finance your child's or children's education in the future.

Taking on New Student Loans

Whether you're planning on continuing your education or paying for your child's or children's education, you're about to take on a considerably large expense. Depending on the college or university and the length of time it takes to graduate, you could be looking at a final bill of anywhere from $30,000 to $200,000 or more.

To pay for a postsecondary education, you have a handful of options, including the following:

- Use your savings and investments.
- Use your current income.
- Tap into the equity in your home. You can do this by doing a cash-out refinance or obtaining a home equity loan or line of credit. There could be tax benefits to doing this rather than using financing options.
- Obtain government grants and scholarships. This is money that you do not need to pay back.
- Obtain private grants and scholarships. This is money that you do not need to pay back.
- Take out government-secured student loans. These loans typically have a lower interest rate and lower fees than other types of loans.

- Take out private loans. These loans typically have a higher interest rate and stricter rules for paying them back. Citibank is one example of a large bank that offers private student loans (*studentloan.citibank.com/slcsite*).

- Use a loan forgiveness program. This type of program pays off student loans if the student, after graduation, does volunteer work, serves in the military, teaches, or provides child care, depending on the program. Loan forgiveness programs apply typically only to student loans secured through the Federal Family Education Loan Program.

- Enlist in the U.S. military. Several programs pay for college education in exchange for military service. Obviously, this involves risk, especially during times of war.

To learn more about potential ways of paying for postsecondary education, including the pros and cons of each method from a financial standpoint, visit the FinAid Page Web site (*www.finaid.org*). According to this Web site, "Parents should expect to pay at least half to two-thirds of their children's college costs through a combination of savings, current income, and loans. Gift aid from the government, the colleges and universities, and private scholarships accounts for only about a third of total college costs."

SMART-DEBT STRATEGY

Thousands of grants and scholarships are available based on merit and special interests as well as financial need. Finding all of the grants and scholarships for which the student in question (whether you or your child) could qualify and then applying for them are an extremely time-consuming process, but the time and effort could save you a lot of money down the road.

Start with a published directory of scholarships. You'll find these directories at your local bookstore or library. You can also research this information online. FastWeb.com (*www.fastweb.com*), Scholarships.com (*www.scholarships.com*), and Scholarship Experts (*www.scholarshipexperts.com*) are three online databases containing thousands of scholarship sources.

Also, be sure to contact the financial aid department of the school the student will be attending for information about scholarships and grants offered directly through the school.

Grants and scholarships are available from a wide range of organizations, businesses, and nonprofit groups. Some are granted based on

---

Smart Debt 101 and Your Student Loans

accomplishments or merit. Others are granted based on need. Many are offered to students with special interests or who belong to a minority. Scholarships are also available to people of specific races, sexual orientation, or religious affiliations, for example.

Every time a student applies for a grant or scholarship, he or she will need to complete a separate application. Before completing an application, make sure the amount of the potential grant or scholarship is worthwhile. Don't waste hours completing a scholarship application where the maximum award is $50 or $100. Pursue scholarships that can really help subsidize the education.

Ideally, if you plan to pay for your child's education, your best bet is to start saving early—like when the child is born. Saving $200 per month from the child's birth to his or her 17th birthday could add up to over $80,000 or more, depending on how you're investing the money.

According to the FinAid Web site, "Paying for college before your child matriculates definitely costs much less than paying for college afterward. Saving $200 a month for ten years at 7% interest would yield $34,818.89. Borrowing the same amount at 6.8% interest with a ten-year term would require payments of $400.70 a month. At 8.5% interest the payments increase to $431.70 a month. (If your return on investment is 4% instead of 7%, you'd accumulate $29,548.13. Borrowing this amount at 6.8% interest would entail monthly payments of $340.04; at 8.5% interest the monthly payments would be $366.35. If your return on investment is 10%, you'd accumulate $41,310.40, corresponding to monthly payments of $475.40 at 6.8% and $512.19 at 8.5%.) So if you elect to borrow instead of saving, you will be paying 1.7 to 2.6 times as much per month."

From a smart-debt standpoint, it's always less expensive to save for an education than to take out loans. Obviously, the least expensive option is for the student to land a full scholarship, but even for straight-A students who are also stellar athletes, for example, this isn't a sure thing.

SMART-DEBT STRATEGY

There are tax benefits to saving money in a special college education savings plan or prepaid tuition plan. Consult with your financial planner or accountant to learn about these plans, especially if you plan to start saving for a child's education when he or she is still young.

44

An Introduction to Student Loans

Student loans, unlike scholarships or grants, must be repaid with interest. To pay for an education, there are three basic types of loans—*student loans* (these include Stafford and Perkins loans), *parent loans* (these include PLUS Loans), and *private loans* (also known as *alternative student loans,* available from banks and other lenders). There are also consolidation loans that allow students to combine all of their loans into one single loan (ideally at a lower interest rate) in order to make only one monthly payment.

More than 75 percent of all college students graduate with some type of debt from student loans. Relying exclusively on grants, scholarships, work-study programs, and other forms of aid that do not require repayment probably won't cover all of the costs.

The good news is that loans granted by the federal government offer lower rates and better repayment plans that most consumer loans. Plus, it's somewhat easier to qualify for them. Up to $2,500 per year in student loan interest is also tax-deductible.

FREE APPLICATION FOR FEDERAL STUDENT AID (FAFSA)

The first step in learning about your options is to visit the official Free Application For Federal Student Aid (FAFSA) Web site (*www.fafsa.ed.gov*) or complete the written application. This should be done every year the student plans to attend school, whether or not you believe the student qualifies for financial aid.

The FAFSA forms and application are available from high schools, colleges, and universities or by calling (800) 4-FED-AID. You can also complete this application online at *www.fafsa.ed.gov*. This is a time-consuming process, so allow at least two to three hours to complete the forms. When completing the forms, have your most recent tax return in hand. If you're a parent paying for a child's education, you'll need the tax returns of both the parent(s) and the student.

After you complete and submit the FAFSA form, your eligibility for all state and federal grants, scholarship money, and loans will be determined automatically. Be sure to visit the Web site to know the deadline for submitting the form for each academic year. Additional information about FAFSA can be found at *www.fafsa.org/fafsa/fafsa.phtml*.

STAFFORD LOANS

The main group of federal loans for students is called *Stafford Loans*. A Stafford Loan is a government-guaranteed loan at low interest rates and with deferred payment options. Students or parents apply for Stafford Loans directly through the FAFSA program.

The Federal Family Education Loan Program (FFELP) guarantees loans provided by private lenders, such as banks or credit unions. Because these loans are guaranteed against default by the federal government, the lenders are willing to offer students or their parents lower interest rates and better loan terms than for other types of unsecured loans. They also don't rely too heavily on credit scores for approval.

The Federal Direct Student Loan Program (FDSLP) provides loans that are administered by participating "direct lending schools." These are loans from the U.S. government that are issued directly to students and/or their parents.

There are two types of Stafford Loans—subsidized or unsubsidized. If a loan is subsidized, it means the government will pay the interest on the loan while the student is in school. These loans are granted based on financial need. If a loan is unsubsidized, the student can defer interest payments until after graduation. The government has imposed strict limits on the amount of money that can be borrowed each year. This amount typically does not cover the entire cost of tuition and other educational expenses.

PERKINS LOANS

Another federal loan is the *Perkins Loan*, which is available to students at the undergraduate and graduate level and is awarded based on financial need. The college or university acts as the lender, using funds provided by the federal government. The Perkins Loan is probably the best type of student loan. It's subsidized (so the government pays the interest while the student is in school) and graduates have a nine-month grace period before they must start making payments on the loan. It has a guaranteed low interest rate (around five percent) and the repayment period is ten years. There is a limit on the amount that can be borrowed each year. The application process for a Perkins Loan is also done through the FAFSA program.

PARENT LOANS

With Stafford and Perkins Loans, the student is the primary borrower. These loans are based less on the student's credit score and credit history and more on his or her financial need and other criteria.

Parents can also take out government loans to help their children pay for college. These are called *Parent Loans*. The Federal Parent Loan for Undergraduate Students (PLUS) program allows parents to borrow money for their child's college education to supplement any loans, grants, and scholarship which the student obtains. In many situations, through PLUS loans students can cover the entire cost of their education.

With a PLUS loan, the parent is the primary borrower, which means that the loan appears on the parent's credit report and impacts his or her credit score. The parent also is responsible for paying back the loan. There is no limit on the amount that parents can borrow with a PLUS loan. As of July 2006, graduate and professional students could also use Parent Loans to pay for their education.

PLUS loans are unsubsidized. The interest rate as of July 2006 is about 8.5 percent. In addition to interest charges, there's a loan fee of four percent. Repayment of the loan begins 60 days after the funds are fully disbursed. The repayment term is ten years.

PRIVATE EDUCATION LOANS

Private education loans are in no way guaranteed against default by the federal government. Thus, the interest rates and fees are typically higher. Plus, approval is based heavily on the applicant's credit history and credit score. If a student does not qualify for a private education loan, a parent or anyone else with good credit can co-sign. This makes both parties fully responsible for repaying the loan.

Private education loans are available from a wide range of banks, credit unions, and other financial institutions. These loans are often used to pay whatever costs are not covered by grants, scholarships, Stafford, Perkins, and/or PLUS loans. Because these loans cost more, they're not ideal for a smart-debt strategy to pay for an education. However, in some cases, these loans are a student's last resort.

Smart Debt 101 and Your Student Loans

If you own a home, determine if it makes better financial sense to pursue a cash-out refinance or apply for a home equity loan or a home equity line of credit instead of applying for a private education loan. You may qualify for better terms than with a private education loan and ultimately save money. A partial list of banks and financial institutions that offer private student loans can be found at *www.fafsa.org/loans/privatestudentloans.phtml*.

SMART-DEBT STRATEGY

A smart-debt approach to paying for a college education dictates that you should use private education loans only if you have already gone through all other, less expensive options, including grants, scholarships, and government-backed loans. If you need to take out a private education loan, shop around for the best possible deal—just as you would for any other types of loan. Also, make sure you'll be able to afford the additional monthly payment(s) you'll be making. Down the road, consider looking into a consolidation loan to reduce the interest rate and fees. To learn more about consolidation loan options related to student loans, visit *www.fafsa.org/ loans/privateconsolidation.phtml*.

To help you make sense of all your options for paying for postsecondary education, consider sitting down with an accountant or financial planner. With a little research you can find experts who specialize in student loans and financial planning to pay for an education. While the obvious priority is to finance an education, it's also important to consider the long-term costs of student loans and other financing options.

SMART-DEBT STRATEGY

On the FinAid Web site, you will find a handful of free online calculators to help you calculate education costs and develop a plan for paying them. These calculators can be found at *www.fafsa.org/calculators*.

Advice for the Student

If you are or will be attending a college or university thanks to student loans that must be paid back after graduation, plan accordingly. Focus on a major that will help you land a high-paying job upon graduation. When you choose your major, understand exactly how it will help you pursue a career that interests you and help to qualify you for the job market. Also, while in

125

school, take full advantage of internships to gain valuable on-the-job training and real-world work experience. A huge percentage of students who perform well in an internship are offered a job, when they graduate, by the company where they interned.

Participating in internships can also help you pinpoint your professional interests and expose you to a wide range of job or career opportunities while you're still in school. Graduating with work experience as well as a degree will give you a big advantage when your job search begins. If you can graduate with a job, you'll be starting the rest of your life in a much better financial position. You'll also be able to pay off your student loans faster and cover all of your everyday living expenses.

If you have student loans, almost immediately after graduating you'll be responsible for making monthly payments. These will be in addition to all of your regular living expenses, car payment, credit card bills, etc. Thus, it's definitely in your best interest to develop a plan for managing these bills and earning as much as possible immediately upon graduation.

*　*　*

In the next chapter, we'll explore many ways to better control your everyday spending, cut costs, and manage your checking and savings accounts. As you'll discover, you should apply smart-debt principles to your everyday spending and money management habits.

CHAPTER 8 | Managing Your Money Using Smart-Debt Principles

An important strategy for adopting smart-debt principles is to avoid accumulating debt. There are basic things you can start doing immediately to:

- Save money on everyday expenses
- Manage your money better
- Increase your income
- Reduce your need to take on new debt
- Pay off your current debt more efficiently

By focusing on these five basics in your everyday finances, not only will you save significant money in the short and long terms, but you'll also be able to reduce the debt you accumulate. You'll be surprised how saving a few dollars here and there can make a big difference, without compromising your quality of life.

Of course, if you're already in serious debt and living well beyond your means, it will be necessary not just to reduce many expenses, but to cut some out completely, which very well could affect your quality of life, at least in the short term.

This chapter offers strategies for managing your money better, reducing everyday living expenses, and potentially increasing your income over the long term. The first step in this process is to determine exactly how you are spending your money. After your paycheck gets deposited into your bank account, what happens to that money? Why is it that, by the end of the month, your bank account is depleted?

To better understand exactly how you're spending your money, it's important to develop a budget for yourself (and your family, if you have one). Then, you'll need to commit to sticking to that budget. This will require a tremendous amount of willpower and focus, especially if you're forced to deal with unexpected expenses.

After developing your budget, you'll want to pick it apart carefully, analyze each and every expense, and determine simple ways to reduce your expenses. Later in this chapter, you'll find a handful of easy cost-cutting measures you can implement to start saving money immediately.

From previous chapters, you already know that it's not smart debt to use credit cards to pay for everyday expenses and then take a lot of time to pay off those debts. This dramatically increases the cost of those expenses, because you're now paying interest, finance charges, and other fees, while you're increasing your debt. If you're in the habit of relying on credit cards, it's important to change that habit immediately and learn how to better manage your income (the cash you have on hand each month).

Adopting smart-debt principles for your everyday expenses involves doing the following:

- Find the least expensive way to purchase products and services you need by shopping around for the best deals.
- Use credit to buy only when it's absolutely necessary and then make sure you'll be able to pay the monthly expenses associated with the additional debt.
- When you use credit, take advantage of credit cards, loans, or financing with the best interest rates and the lowest fees possible.
- Make only necessary purchases.
- Develop a plan to pay for your purchases immediately, before making them.
- Establish a detailed budget for your everyday living expenses—and then stick to it.

- Make a point of paying off your current debt, without taking on new debt each month.
- Develop an emergency fund to cover unexpected expenses, such as car repairs, home repairs, or medical bills, so you aren't forced to use your high-interest credit cards and accumulate more debt.
- Focus on protecting your credit rating and credit score at all times. One way to do this is to pay all of your bills (including your mortgage, car loan, and credit card bills) on time.

The deeper into financial trouble you slide, the more fees and the more interest you'll be paying, a cycle that often becomes an endless spiral of owing more and paying more. If you're short on cash and bounce a few checks, you'll be paying hefty fees. If you're late in paying a credit card bill or go slightly over your credit limit, you'll be paying extra fees. If you don't maintain a minimum balance as required for your checking or savings account, you'll be paying extra fees.

As you attempt to apply smart-debt principles to your everyday spending, one of the best things to start doing right away is taking steps to avoid and eliminate all of the extra fees you're paying to your bank, credit card issuers, and other financial institutions. Simply by better managing your money, you can avoid overdraft fees, over-limit fees, and ATM fees, for example—all of which can add up to hundreds of dollars per month.

Create a Budget and Stick to It

Back in Chapter 1, you completed Worksheet #3, a summary of your monthly expenses. In order to create a detailed budget, you need to identify which of your month-to-month expenses are absolutely necessary and then list all of your other expenses in order to get a clear picture of how you're spending your money.

First, make a list of all your current monthly expenses. To ensure that you list everything, refer to your bills, monthly statements, and checkbook. As you list each expense, categorize it by its importance.

- Place a "1" next to all vital expenses that you must pay each month on time. Your rent or mortgage, car loan, alimony and/or child support, student loans, insurance, and credit card bills are examples of mandatory expenses.
- Place a "2" next to all expenses that are important, but not critical to

your survival or your standard of living. Examples might include your cable TV bill and health club membership.

- Place a "3" next to expenses that are optional, totally discretionary. These expenses are not at all necessary, but enhance your quality of life. Examples might include entertainment, coffee and snacks, Internet access, gifts, and dining out.

Expense Type	Priority (1 = mandatory) (2 = important) (3 = optional)	Monthly Amount ($)	Annual Amount ($)	How Could This Expense Be Reduced or Eliminated?
Alimony and/or Child Support				
Automobile Club Membership				
Babysitting				
Cable TV, TiVo, and/or Satellite Radio				
Car Insurance				
Car Maintenance				
Car Payment				
Cell Phone				
Cigarettes / Tobacco				
Clothing				
Coffee/Snacks				
Cosmetics				
Credit Card(s)				
Daycare				
Dining Out / Restaurants				
Entertainment				

Worksheet 8-1. Personal or family expenses (continued on next page)

Managing Your Money Using Smart-Debt Principles

Expense Type	Priority (1 = mandatory) (2 = important) (3 = optional)	Monthly Amount ($)	Annual Amount ($)	How Could This Expense Be Reduced or Eliminated?
Food and Other Groceries				
Fuel (for your Car)				
Gifts				
Gym/Health Club Member-ship				
Health Insurance				
Home Telephone and Fax				
Homeowner's or Renter's Insurance				
Household Items				
Housekeeper				
Internet Access				
Landscaper				
Life Insurance				
Memberships				
Other Insurance				
Pet Grooming and Daycare				
Postage				
Prescriptions				
Real Estate Taxes				
Rent or Mortgage				
Student Loan(s)				
Tolls and Parking				

Worksheet 8-1. Personal or family expenses (continued on next page)

Expense Type	Priority (1 = mandatory) (2 = important) (3 = optional)	Monthly Amount ($)	Annual Amount ($)	How Could This Expense Be Reduced or Eliminated?
Travel				
Electricity				
Natural Gas				
Water				
Vet Bills and Pet Insurance				
Other				
Other				
Other				
Total Expenses:		$	$	

Worksheet 8-1. Personal or family expenses (continued)

One of the first steps toward reducing your monthly expenses and developing a workable budget is to focus on all of the expenses you categorized as "optional" (3). How can you cut these expenses or totally eliminate them from your budget?

Figure out what expenses are absolutely unnecessary and cut them out of your budget altogether. Next, figure out how to reduce the expenses for other items you identified as "optional." For example, if you stop at Starbucks every morning on your way to work, could you instead make coffee at home and save $3 to $5 per day? If you smoke cigarettes, could you cut down? If you're a member of a gym or a health club, could you find one that's less expensive or a less expensive membership option? If you have cable TV, could you sign up for fewer premium channels and pay for only HBO, Showtime, or Cinemax instead of all three premium movie channels? Would satellite TV be less expensive than cable TV?

You'll be surprised how much money you can save simply by reducing or eliminating some of your optional expenses. If you reduce each of these expenses by just a few dollars per month, the annual savings will be significant. This is money that you can use to pay off debt faster, save, invest, or use to improve your quality of life. For example, if you make just one extra mortgage payment per year toward your principal, you'll save tens of thousands of dollars over the term of your mortgage and pay it off significantly faster. Likewise, paying just $50 per month more than now on your credit card bills will pay off that outstanding debt faster and save a lot in interest, finance charges, and fees over the long term.

The money you save from your budget could also be used to establish and maintain an emergency fund, so you have cash available for unexpected expenses, such as emergency car repairs, home repairs, and medical bills.

SMART-DEBT STRATEGY

When buying something, don't just think in terms of what it will cost today or what your monthly payment will be if you use credit or financing. Focus on the total cost over time. Crunch the numbers and you may figure out that buying the item with a credit card and then taking one, two, three, or more years to pay it off is not smart. In some cases, you may even discover you'll still be paying for the item long after you've used it up, worn it out, or replaced it. For example, taking five years to pay for a home computer doesn't make sense when you'll most likely need to replace it in less than two or three years. If you pay 18 percent interest on your credit card and you spend $2,500 on a computer, if you make only the minimum monthly payments, it'll take you 244 months (20 years!) to pay off the computer, plus you'll be paying $3,365.51 in interest charges. The computer will be out-of-date and need to be replaced long before it's paid off.

Follow the same procedure for expenses you listed as important, but not mandatory (2). Many of these probably can't be eliminated altogether, but you can probably find ways to reduce them. For example, to cut your clothing budget, perhaps you can shop for sale items or shop at designer outlet stores more often, instead of major department stores or high-priced clothing boutiques. Many stores and outlets sell top-brand designer clothing at reduced prices.

Finding ways to reduce your important expenses will require you to tap your creativity, shop around, and become a more educated consumer. One strategy, for example, is to buy items that will last longer and that are better made, so they won't need to be replaced as soon or as often.

As you evaluate your mandatory expenses, you may find ways to reduce these too, even though you cannot totally eliminate them. For example, if you own your home, could you save money by refinancing your mortgage? Could you shop around for lower insurance rates? Could you reduce your utility bills by keeping the heat a few degrees lower in the winter and using the air conditioner less in the summer? You could also replace your traditional light bulbs with energy-efficient bulbs that require less electricity and last longer. Perhaps adding more insulation in your home would lower your utility costs.

Once you develop a budget you can live with and that covers all of your mandatory expenses and important expenses, without having to tap into your savings or rely on credit cards, you must become disciplined and stick to this budget. One of the biggest ways people waste money is by buying things they don't need, simply because they're on sale. An easy way to help avoid this temptation is to make a shopping list before each visit to the supermarket or mall. If you want to buy something that's not on your list as being absolutely necessary, don't do it. Refrain from spontaneous purchases or impulse buying! Learning to control your spending impulse will play a huge role in your ability to stick to your budget.

Another important strategy is to become more aware of managing your checking account. It's easy to make lots of purchases using your ATM card and not focus on how much you're spending. With telephone and online banking, it's easy to get real-time balances for your account(s) and carefully monitor your spending habits. Get into the habit of checking your account balances every day and knowing exactly how you're spending your money.

Each time you're about to buy something, ask yourself the following questions:

- How important is it that I buy this product or service right now? On my expense report, how would I categorize this purchase, as mandatory, important, or optional?
- Can I afford this purchase?
- How will I pay for this purchase? If I'm using a credit card or financing it, how quickly will I be able to pay off the debt? How much extra will the purchase cost if I have to pay interest and finance charges? Is it still worth it?
- How will I use this product or service? How will it improve my quality of life?
- What happens if I don't purchase this product or service?
- How does making the purchase impact my budget?
- Am I getting the absolute best price on this product or service? By shopping around, could I buy it for less elsewhere? Could I save money by buying it online? Could I use a coupon or wait for the item to go on sale in order to save money?

- What type of warranty, guarantee, or money-back offer comes with this product or service?

Reduce Your Banking Fees

Banks have discovered countless ways to charge for services that in the past were free. Many savings accounts come with a monthly maintenance fee if you don't maintain a minimum balance; some even charge extra to make deposits and withdrawals. For checking accounts, there can be monthly maintenance fees, overdraft fees, check writing fees, ATM fees, bounced check fees, fees for using a bank teller, fees associated with ordering checks, fees to use online banking, and fees to use telephone banking. If you're not careful, these fees can amount to $100 or more every month. This is money you don't necessarily have to be spending.

When managing your bank accounts, first shop around banks, credit unions, savings and loans, and other financial institutions for the best deals. If a bank offers "free checking," read the fine print to make sure that the account is really 100 percent free or a $5,000 balance is required or there's a monthly fee. Also, find out what charges and fees apply, especially if you'll be using an ATM card with the account.

Once you find a bank that doesn't go out of its way to charge its customers an insane number of fees just to maintain a basic checking or savings account, apply another smart-debt principle—manage the account properly. Keep careful track of your balance, so you don't bounce checks or overspend and incur overdraft charges. At many banks, if you use your ATM or debit card and spend beyond your balance by even $1, you could be hit with an overdraft fee of $20 or more. If you know you get charged for using an ATM that's outside of your bank's ATM network, refrain from using those ATMs and save the service charge of $1 to $3 per usage. These are actions you can take in managing your account that will save you money.

Local banks, credit unions, savings and loans, and other financial institutions all want you to do your banking with them. In addition to the fees they'll charge, here are some other things to consider when shopping for a bank (to use the term generically):

- How many branches does the bank have near where you live, work, and spend most of your time?
- When are the local branches open? Many banks now have extended hours during the week and are open on weekends.

- How many ATMs does the bank have and where are they located? With what nationwide ATM networks is the bank affiliated? What fees apply if you use an ATM that's not owned and operated by your bank?
- Does the bank offer all of the services you'll want and need, beyond checking and/or savings accounts? What about credit cards, loans, investment opportunities, safe deposit boxes, online banking, telephone banking, and 24-hour telephone customer service? Does the bank offer competitive rates for these services?
- Are deposits in the bank insured by the FDIC?
- For its checking accounts, does the bank limit the number of checks a customer can write each month? Is there a minimum balance that a customer must maintain? Is there a limit on the number of withdrawals or deposits per month?
- What interest rate does the bank offer on its accounts? Can this rate automatically change after an account is opened? Does the bank pay different interest rates based on the balance in an account? How is the interest calculated?
- How good is the bank's customer service? How long do customers typically wait in line for a teller or other representative? Is the staff friendly, knowledgeable, and helpful? Is the telephone customer service readily available and helpful?

Finding a financial institution that can handle all of your banking needs, without charging you a fortune in fees, may be a challenge. You'll probably need to visit a handful of banks and shop around for the best deals. Unfortunately, once you establish a primary checking account, it's a hassle to close the account and move your money to another bank, so you should plan to stay for a while with whichever bank you choose.

Types of Bank Accounts

When it comes to storing any money you save, you have many options. There are traditional savings accounts available from banks, credit unions, savings and loan associations, and other financial institutions. There is also a wide range of investment opportunities, ranging from CDs and money market accounts to savings bonds, Treasury Bills, stocks, bonds, and mutual funds. Within financial institutions, you'll find a variety of options for services—and a variety of fees associated with those services. Which option you choose will depend on a variety of factors, including the following:

- What your goals are for the money
- How much risk you're willing to assume (if you're investing)
- How long you have to achieve your financial goals with that money
- What type of access you want in terms of withdrawing your money and/or managing your accounts
- How much interest you'd like to earn (putting your money to work for you, earning interest, is definitely smart debt, since it's the opposite of debt and paying interest)

SAVINGS ACCOUNTS

A traditional *savings account* allows you to earn interest on your money. The rate will be relatively low, however. Some banks provide savings account holders with an ATM card so they can more easily manage their accounts. In many cases, a savings account can also be linked to a checking account with the same bank, so transferring funds between accounts is fast and simple, in person, by telephone, or online. Unless you maintain a specified minimum balance in your savings account, you'll probably be charged a monthly maintenance fee.

A *passbook savings account* provides you with a book that you present to the teller every time you make a deposit or withdrawal, as identification and so he or she can record the transaction. These days, a much more common form of savings account is a *statement savings account*. The bank provides you with a monthly statement listing all of your banking transactions. In some cases, these statements can also be accessed online.

The amount of interest you'll earn on a deposit will be based on the annual percentage yield offered by the bank. The bank must provide this information along with a list of all fees associated with the account.

SMART-DEBT STRATEGY

You must determine if the balance you'll maintain in your savings account and the annual percentage yield will be high enough to earn more interest than the bank will charge in fees for that account.

CHECKING ACCOUNTS

For being able to spend your money, a full-service checking account that includes an ATM/debit card and online banking services will probably be the most useful. However, it's important to manage this type of account carefully to avoid excessive charges, especially when writing checks and using your ATM/debit card. A typical checking account allows you to withdraw money from the account by writing a check, visiting the bank, or using an ATM machine. You can also use your debit card (instead of a check) to make purchases and the funds for each purchase will automatically (and almost immediately) be transferred from your checking account.

Your bank may or may not pay interest on money in your checking account. The fees you will pay will vary greatly, as will the services available to you through your account. As you're shopping around, decide in advance which services you want from your checking account and then visit a handful of banks and other financial institutions to find the best options available.

The services available to you may be limited based on your credit score. For example, most banks and other financial institutions will not offer overdraft protection to customers with below-average credit scores. Also, if you have a history of bouncing checks or closing accounts with other banks without covering bounced checks and overdrafts, you may have difficulty opening an account with any bank. The size of the balance you plan to keep in the account may also determine what services are offered to you. Some banks and other financial institutions require account holders to maintain a minimum balance in order to avoid additional fees or to keep the account open.

These are some of the services you should look for when opening a checking account:

- No (or extremely low) monthly maintenance fees
- No minimum balance requirement or a minimum you know you'll be able to maintain easily
- Free checks and unlimited check-writing privileges
- Free ATM/debit card with unlimited free transactions at ATMs within the bank's network
- Free online banking and bill paying
- Free in-person teller assistance when making a deposit or a withdrawal
- Free telephone banking services and 24-hour customer assistance
- Direct deposit (if applicable)
- Overdraft protection (with funds automatically transferred from your savings account at no fee)

One of the most common ways checking account holders rack up significant (and often unnecessary) fees is by causing their balance to dip

Managing Your Money Using Smart-Debt Principles

SMART-DEBT STRATEGY

Many banks will reduce the fees associated with maintaining a checking account if you sign up to have your paycheck automatically deposited into your account by your employer. This is called *direct deposit*.

---

below zero. They write checks, they use ATMs, they have their bills paid automatically—and they don't track the money leaving their account so they don't realize when the balance is getting too low. Each time your balance goes negative, the bank will charge you an overdraft fee. You may also be charged a "bounced check fee" or "non-sufficient funds" fee if the bank returns your check without paying it. These fees can cost you $20, $30, or even $60 or more per incident, depending on the financial institution and the fees charged by the merchant that didn't get any money from your check.

The easiest way to avoid these fees is to keep track of your balance and take into account all of the banking fees and automatic bill payments that will be withdrawn from the account each month. Also, don't forget about ATM fees, ATM cash withdrawals, and purchases you make with your debit card.

Aside from carefully monitoring your account balance, you could also sign up for overdraft protection. This is a type of loan for which your credit score must qualify you. If you use overdraft protection, you could wind up paying an extra fee, plus interest. Some banks offer overdraft protection that automatically transfers sums from your savings account to cover checks or debit card purchases, for example. The fees associated with this service also vary.

Using overdraft protection as a form of short-term loan to cover your bills or to obtain quick cash when you're in a financial bind can become costly. It's better to have overdraft protection only as insurance against miscalculations, but not to rely on it to help cover your expenses, since the interest charged by financial institutions is typically as high as for a credit card, if not higher. According to *The New York Times*, one of the largest financial institutions in the United States recently charged in excess of $1 billion in overdraft fees in a single year. It is also considered one of the most aggressive in promoting overdraft protection. Overdraft plans, which may charge fees as high as $35 per overdraft, are essentially high-interest short-term loans—and there's no legal limit on the percentage return they get from those loans. Do the math!

Take advantage of online banking and telephone banking and then carefully review your printed monthly statements. That will help you keep track of your balance and better manage your account.

SMART-DEBT STRATEGY

Use your ATM card only at ATMs that are affiliated with your bank and don't charge an extra fee. Using an ATM outside of your bank's network could cost anywhere from $1 to $5 per transaction. If you're traveling, you often cannot avoid these fees, but around home, stick to using your bank's ATM network.

MONEY MARKET ACCOUNTS

Another popular type of account is a *money market account*. These accounts pay interest and typically allow account holders to write checks in order to access their funds. These accounts usually require the account holder to maintain a minimum balance and they usually limit the number of deposits or withdrawals that can be made each month. A money market account is a very low-risk investment account that pays higher interest than a traditional savings or checking account. It's a better alternative to a certificate of deposit (CD), because you can withdraw your funds at any time with no penalty. These accounts are also fully insured by the Federal Deposit Insurance Corporation (FDIC), just like savings accounts. To open a money market account, an initial deposit of between $1,000 and $5,000 will typically be required.

SMART DEBT STRATEGY

If you have several thousand dollars in a traditional savings account, those funds can earn higher interest if you transfer them into a money market account. This account works best if you won't need access to your money quickly, but don't want to risk investing in stocks or mutual funds, for example.

CERTIFICATE OF DEPOSIT (CD) ACCOUNTS

A *certificate of deposit* (CD) is another form of savings plan offered by many banks and other financial institutions. A CD pays a higher interest rate than a savings account; however, you have to make a predetermined minimum deposit to obtain a CD and then leave the money in the account for a predetermined period, ranging from six months to several years. The size of the deposit and the length of the CD will determine your interest rate. This is a totally safe investment; however, there is a financial penalty if you withdraw your funds before the CD's maturity date. A money market account does not have this early withdrawal penalty.

SMART DEBT STRATEGY

When choosing a bank or other financial institution, make sure it's a *federally insured depository institution*. This means that the Federal Deposit Insurance Corporation (FDIC), an independent agency created by Congress in 1933, protects your savings up to a limit of $100,000. Checking, savings, and CDs are typically covered automatically, but make sure that this free insurance covers your type(s) of account. To learn more, visit the FDIC's Web site (*www.fdic.gov*) or call (877) ASK-FDIC (275-3342).

Payday Lending Is Not Smart Debt!

Payday loans are advertised as being a fast and convenient way to obtain a short-term, unsecured cash loan, typically for less than $1,000. You'll see ads for payday loans everywhere and find check-cashing stores everywhere offering them.

To get this type of loan, typically you write a check and date it for your next payday. The lender charges a flat fee plus interest on the loan. You may pay anywhere from $10 to $30 (or more) for every $100 cashed, even if the loan period is only a few days. This translates to an APR of 300, 400, or even 1,000 percent. In other words, using a payday loan should in no way be considered smart debt. Payday loans are like credit card cash advances: high fees and interest charges for short-term loans.

If you get need emergency cash more than once every few years, chances are you're somehow mismanaging your money. Relying on high-interest loans only leads to increased debt and extra fees, finance charges, and interest—money that you could put to much better use.

SMART-DEBT STRATEGY

Payday loans and check-cashing services work slightly differently, yet both are expensive and should only be used in an emergency, if absolutely necessary. Using either of these services would not be considered a smart-debt strategy, because the fees and interest charged are too high.

Cut Everyday Expenses

You probably spend money on a wide range of products and services. Some of these purchases are absolutely necessary. Others are less critical. Some are totally frivolous. As you develop your budget and begin coming up with ways to cut expenses, focus on categories of expenses. This section offers some easy tips for saving money on automotive, clothing, grocery, home improvement, insurance, travel, and utilities.

As a general rule, you can save money by doing the following:

- Shopping for the best deals and being price-conscious
- Waiting for sales
- Using coupons and other money-saving offers on products and services you need
- Shopping at discount and outlet stores

TAKE ADVANTAGE OF PRICE-COMPARISON WEB SITES

Using the Internet, you can quickly compare prices for products and services from dozens of merchants and then make purchases online or be directed to a local store. Use price-comparison Web sites. Simply enter the exact product you're looking to purchase (including the manufacturer, make and model, as appropriate) and then review the search results for the lowest prices.

There are dozens of price-comparison shopping Web sites that cost nothing to use and allow you to search for literally thousands of products. These sites include:

- **NexTag.com** (*www.nextag.com*)
- **BizRate.com** (*www.bizrate.com*)
- **PriceGrabber.com** (*www.pricegrabber.com*)
- **bottomdollar.com** (*www.bottomdollar.com*)
- **Shopzilla.com** (*www.shopzilla.com*)
- **Shopping.com** (*www.shopping.com*)

There are also price-comparison Web sites for specific products or services, like mortgages and refinancing (*www.bankrate.com* and *lendingtree.com*). One popular service for finding the best rates for insurance, credit cards, long-distance phone service, and cellular service is LowerMyBills.com (*www.lowermybills.com*). For new and used cars, Vehix.com (*www.vehix.com*) and CarTrader.com (*www.cartrader.com*) are two excellent price-comparison Web sites.

MORE MONEY-SAVING STRATEGIES ANYONE CAN IMPLEMENT

You can also compare prices for services and save money on various expenses by shopping around for better deals at other stores or vendors. For health insurance, auto insurance, homeowner's/renter's insurance, and life insurance, for example, you can contact several agents and brokers, have them analyze your current policies and coverage, and then recommend how you can save money. Often, when you use the same broker to purchase multiple types of insurance policies, you'll save even more.

Did you know that the average U.S. household spends more than $1,600 per year on energy bills? With energy prices rising, heating and cooling a home, for example, has become extremely costly.

To save on your utility bills, contact your electric and gas provider and see if they offer free in-home inspections. An energy expert will check your home from roof to basement and identify where you could make free or very inexpensive improvements to save energy. For example, they might recommend adding insulation in your attic, sealing drafty windows and doors, or using energy-efficient light bulbs. To learn more about saving money by insulating better, visit the EnergySavers.gov Web site (*www.energysavers.gov*).

There are also energy-efficient major appliances that will help you save money on your energy bills. Look for appliances with the Energy Star logo. These appliances and products meet strict efficiency guidelines developed by the U.S. Environmental Protection Agency and the U.S. Department of Energy. To learn more about the Energy Star program, visit *www.energystar. gov*. This organization also offers free home energy-conservation evaluations in many areas throughout the country. On the Energy Star Web site are dozens of strategies for cutting your energy bills. For example, properly cleaning and maintaining your major appliances will you save money and keep them operating at peak efficiency.

This same strategy also works with your automobile. Keeping it properly maintained will ensure the highest gas mileage possible. Be sure to check with your dealership or mechanic to determine if changing the type of oil you use in your car will improve your fuel efficiency. Whenever you visit a service station, take a few minutes to check the air pressure in your tires. Keeping your tires properly inflated can improve gas mileage up to four percent. Also, replacing a clogged air filter can improve gas mileage up to ten percent.

Develop an Emergency Fund

For the first few months after you begin saving by reducing nonessential purchases and expenses, set aside some of that money in a separate savings account that you can call your emergency fund. This is money that you can use for unanticipated expenses. Emergency car repairs or repairs to your home or major appliances, unexpected medical bills, or sudden loss of your job are just some possible reasons for maintaining a "rainy day fund."

Ideally, you'll want to set aside enough money in this fund to cover your living expenses for at least three months, but you can start off with a few hundred dollars and then contribute $50, $100, or more to the account each month. Do not tap into these funds for anything other than emergency expenses. Wanting to purchase a new big-screen TV or take a vacation does not qualify as an emergency.

* * *

Now you understand why creating, managing, and sticking to a budget is important, you know ways to save money on your monthly expenses, and you've created a plan to put some of your money to better use. The next chapter focuses getting the professional help you might need to identify and fix financial problems. That's the next step to using smart debt.

CHAPTER 9 | Getting the Help You Need to Fix Your Credit and Debt Problems

*T*here are countless reasons why people get into serious debt, max out their credit cards, and simply run out of money. These are some of these reasons:

- Theft or fraud
- Carelessness with money and frivolous spending habits
- Death of a loved one
- Loss of a job
- Not developing a good personal or family budget and sticking to it
- Sudden illness or medical emergency
- Not applying the smart-debt principles outlined in this book

Whatever the reason, people who find themselves experiencing serious financial problems often don't realize it until it's too late. Then, because the problems have gotten so big and out of control, these same people don't know where to begin to fix the situation, so they simply ignore or deny the problems. The problems just get worse.

SMART-DEBT STRATEGY

Every time you take on any new debt, one of the most important smart-debt strategies is first to develop a detailed plan for paying off that debt in a timely manner. Failure to create a repayment plan and then stick to it will eventually lead to financial problems, more debt, more fees, and more interest charges.

Whether it's a result or a cause, increasing debt and poor credit go hand-in-hand with personal financial problems. As you fall behind on monthly payments for loans and credit cards, negative information will begin popping up on your credit reports. Then, your credit score will steadily decline, so the interest rates you're paying on your credit cards and loans will increase. Also, when you attempt to apply for additional credit or loans, first, you will just pay more because your credit score is lower. But then, after more time passes, you'll probably be unable to qualify at all for new loans and credit.

This is the point when many people discover they're in serious financial trouble and don't know where to turn or what to do next. When you start experiencing any type of short-term or long-term financial problems, it's important to begin dealing with them immediately in order to avoid much larger problems down the road.

For example, if you can't make your car loan payment some month, call the creditor and explain your situation and the reason. If the reason is valid, the lender will probably work with you by extending the loan and allowing you to skip a payment or two, restructuring or refinancing the loan at a lower interest rate, waiving interest fees or late charges, or developing another solution with you to keep that loan from causing greater financial hardship.

Especially if you've recently lost your job, experienced a medical emergency, or have some other extenuating circumstance in your personal and financial life, the key to avoiding long-term credit and financial problems is to immediately contact your creditors and lenders and work with them. Don't allow bills to pile up as you skip payments. Ignoring the situation is the worst strategy.

Identifying that you're experiencing financial problems is the first step toward fixing them. Next, it's important to pinpoint the type of financial problems you're experiencing and why. Are your problems a result of excessive credit card debt? Are you living beyond your financial means? Has your income decreased suddenly and dramatically or stopped? Have you been hit by large, unexpected bills, such as costly home repairs or medical needs?

Depending on the nature of your financial problems, you'll want to seek help from professionals with the appropriate expertise. For example, if you need help planning and managing your personal finances, a financial planner or accountant may be most suitable. If you're dealing with credit-related problems, a credit counselor is probably best equipped to help you.

Finding the right type of expert is important. However, you must be willing to accept the advice offered, develop a thoughtful plan to resolve your problems, and then stick to that plan for however long it takes to achieve your goals. Fixing most financial problems takes time. In fact, you may need to adopt a plan that will take three to five years to achieve its objectives, so stick to your plan, be persistent, and stay dedicated.

Money Management Problems? A CPA or CFP Can Probably Help!

In the United States, there are countless people every month who begin experiencing serious financial and credit difficulties, yet don't know where to turn. If you're fortunate to have an accountant, a Certified Public Account (CPA), a financial planner, or a Certified Financial Planner (CFP) with whom you've worked in the past and who is familiar with your financial situation, this is definitely the financial expert to turn to now.

Even if you've never worked with any type of accountant or financial planner, if you can afford to hire one, even for a few hours, to review your current situation and recommend some solutions, this is the fastest and easiest way to begin finding solutions to your financial and credit problems.

When seeking out an accountant or financial planner, look for someone with experience and expertise working with people in your situation, but beware of people advertising themselves as "credit repair experts." Seek out someone with appropriate certification. For example, find a Certified Public Accountant (CPA) instead of just an accountant. If you're seeking out a financial planner, find someone who's a Certified Financial Planner. This will help ensure that the person you hire is qualified, experienced, and reputable.

If you're experiencing credit-related problems, you could also seek guidance from a reputable credit counseling service. While a financial planner can help you with all aspects of money management and budgeting, a credit counselor can do the following:

- Advise you about managing your money and using credit
- Provide strategies for resolving your current financial problems
- Help you create a personalized plan to avoid future difficulties with credit
- Help you negotiate with your creditors and lenders
- Develop and help you implement a debt management plan (DMP) to bail yourself out of your financial predicament

---

SMART-DEBT STRATEGY

The best way to find an accountant or a financial planner is through a referral from someone you know. Otherwise, consider contacting a professional association, such as the Certified Financial Planner Board of Standards (*www.cfp.com/search/*) or the American Institute of Certified Public Accountants (*pfp.aicpa.org/community*).

When you begin working with an accountant, a financial planner, or a credit counselor, the personal and financial information you provide is typically kept confidential, unless you authorize that person to contact and negotiate with your creditors and lenders on your behalf.

Strategies for Finding a Qualified Financial Planner

In America, there are more than 50,000 Certified Financial Planners (people who have earned their CPF certification). On its Web site (*www.cfp.com*), the Certified Financial Planner Board of Standards offers the following advice for finding a qualified financial planner:

1. **Know what you want.** Determine your general financial goals and/ or specific needs (insurance policy analysis, estate planning, investment advice, college tuition financing, etc.) to better focus your search.
2. **Be prepared.** Read personal finance publications (*Worth, Money, SmartMoney, Kiplinger's Personal Finance*, etc.) to become more familiar with financial planning strategies and terminology.
3. **Talk with others.** Get referrals from advisors you trust, business

associates, and friends. Or contact one of the financial planning organizations for a referral to a member in your area.

4. **Look for competence.** Choose a financial planning professional with certification that indicates that he or she is ethical and has met standards of financial planning competency, such as the Certified Financial Planner (CFP) certification.

5. **Interview more than one planner.** Ask the planners to describe their educational backgrounds, experience and specialties, the size and duration of their practice, how often they communicate with clients, and whether an assistant handles client matters. Make sure you feel comfortable discussing your finances with the planner you select.

6. **Check the planner's background**. Depending on the financial planner's area of expertise, call the securities or insurance departments in your state for his or her complaint record. Call the CFP Board toll-free at (888) CFP-MARK (237-6275) or visit *www.cfp.net* to determine if a planner is currently authorized to use the CFP certification marks or has ever been publicly disciplined by the CFP Board.

7. **Know what to expect.** Ask for a registration or disclosure statement (such as a Form ADV, mandatory for advisors required to register with the Securities and Exchange Commission) detailing the planner's compensation methods, conflicts of interest, business affiliations, and personal qualifications.

8. **Get it in writing.** Request a written advisory contract or engagement letter to document the nature and scope of services the planner will provide. You should also understand whether compensation will be fee-based, commission-based, or a combination.

9. **Re-assess the relationship regularly.** Financial planning relationships quite often continue for a long time. Review your professional relationship regularly and ensure that your planner understands your goals and needs as they develop and change over time.

Credit Counselors Are Available to Help You

There are many companies that advertise credit counseling and credit repair services. While you can assume that virtually all companies that promote themselves as "credit repair" companies are not legitimate, it's harder to determine if a credit counseling service is reputable.

SMART-DEBT STRATEGY

Instead of responding to ads on late-night television or the radio, for example, one of the best ways to find a reliable and reputable credit counseling service is to contact the National Foundation for Credit Counseling (800 388-2227, *www.nfcc.org*) for a referral in your area. You'll be provided with free information and have the opportunity to speak with a certified credit counselor who will charge you little or nothing for the consultation.

The National Foundation for Credit Counseling (NFCC), founded in 1951, is the oldest and largest national nonprofit credit counseling organization in the United States. Its mission is to set the national standard for quality credit counseling, debt-reduction services, and education for financial wellness, through its member agencies. Those agencies have trained, certified credit counselors who offer low-cost and free educational information, management advice, and debt-reduction services. NFCC members help more than two million consumers annually through nearly 1,000 agency offices nationwide.

The NFCC Web site offers tools and information to help consumers develop short- and long-term strategies for fixing their credit problems. To learn more, visit the DebtAdvice.org Web site (*www.debtadvice.org*).

By working with a credit counselor, you will be able to develop a practical and individualized plan for paying off your debt. If you have severe debt, you may be eligible to enroll in a debt management plan (DMP), which is a systematic way to pay down debt through monthly deposits to the credit counseling agency, which will then distribute the funds to your creditors. By participating in this type of program, you may benefit from reduced or waived finance charges and fewer collection calls.

It takes approximately 36 to 60 months to repay debts through a DMP. Your accounts with creditors will always be credited with 100 percent of the amount you pay. For those with considerable debt problems, entering into a debt management plan is an effective step in getting out of debt.

The goal of NFCC members is to provide free or affordable services to consumers who need help to get out of serious debt. Some of those members offer free counseling and debt management plan services. Members who charge fees or request contributions offer their personalized services at affordable fees.

In addition to providing one-on-one, personalized service and counseling, many NFCC member agencies also provide free seminars, which are open to the public. For more personalized services, budget counseling is available for as little as $13, while assistance in creating and implementing a complete debt management plan (DMP) comes at a monthly fee averaging below $25.

What sets the NFCC agencies apart from other nonprofit organizations is that it receives funding from sources besides its clients. As a result, while other credit counselors charge high start-up fees and monthly service charges, the NFCC's rates are extremely low and there are no hidden costs.

SMART-DEBT STRATEGY

A credit counseling service can help you create and implement a formal and personalized debt management plan (DMP). According to the Federal Trade Commission, here's how a DMP works.

You deposit money each month with the credit counseling organization. The organization uses your deposits to pay your unsecured debts, like credit card bills, student loans, and medical bills, according to a payment schedule the counselor develops with you and your creditors. Your creditors may agree to lower your interest rates and waive certain fees, but check with all your creditors to be sure that they offer the concessions that a credit counseling organization describes to you. A successful DMP requires you to make regular, timely payments, and could take 48 months or longer to complete. Ask the credit counselor to estimate how long it will take for you to complete the plan. You also may have to agree not to apply for—or use—any additional credit while you're participating in the plan.

Because many companies and individuals fraudulently pass themselves off as credit counselors in order to capitalize on personal financial misfortunes, the Federal Trade Commission (FTC) has developed a list of eight questions to help you determine if a particular credit counseling agency is reputable:

1. *What services are offered?* A reputable credit counseling service will offer budget counseling classes in savings and debt management, plus be able to provide you with the services of someone who is trained and certified in consumer credit and money and debt management. A credit counselor should begin by discussing your personal situation

with you, help you develop a personalized plan to solve your immediate money and credit problems, and then teach you how to avoid such problems in the future. During your first meeting with a credit counselor, be prepared to spend between 60 and 90 minutes analyzing your personal situation.

2. *Is the credit counselor licensed in your state to provide the services being offered?* Many states require counselors to obtain a license before offering credit counseling, debt management plans, or other related services to consumers.

3. *Does the credit counseling service offer free information?* A credit counseling company should never charge for information about the services it offers.

4. *Will you be required to sign a formal contract or agreement with the credit counseling company?* Never agree to pay for any services over the telephone. You should receive a written contract or agreement before a company charges you for credit counseling services or participating in a debt management plan (DMP).

5. *Does the credit counseling agency or service have a good reputation with the Better Business Bureau and your state attorney general?* Check whether any formal complaints have been filed against the company. From the Better Business Bureau Web site (*www.bbb.org*), you can search for complaints against a company and find contact information for your local BBB office. Keep in mind that even if you can't find any complaints against a company, that is not an absolute guarantee that the company is reputable.

6. *How much will the credit counseling services cost?* Obtain a detailed price quote in writing and make sure it lists all of the fees. Determine if there are any upfront or start-up costs, monthly fees, or other charges for services.

7. *How are the individual credit counselors paid?* Are they given a commission based on services you sign up for? According to the FTC, "If the organization will not disclose what compensation it receives from creditors, or how employees are compensated, go elsewhere for help."

8. *Will the credit counselor keep the information you provide confidential?* Who will have access to the personal and financial information you supply?

> ### SMART-DEBT STRATEGY
>
> The Federal Trade Commission publishes free booklets, including *Fiscal Fitness: Choosing a Credit Counselor* and *Knee Deep in Debt*, which can be obtained online at www.ftc.gov/credit or by calling (877) FTC-HELP (382-4357). These booklets provide useful information for hiring a credit counselor, applying for a debt consolidation loan, or filing for bankruptcy.

Beware of Scams

To help you choose a credit counseling or debt negotiation service, the FTC has published a list of behaviors that are often signs of a scam. If a company does any of the following things, *do not* work with those people:

- The company guarantees that your unsecured debt can be erased or removed from your credit report and that the creditors to whom you owe money will simply go away.
- The company promises that unsecured debts can be paid off with pennies on the dollar.
- The company requires a start-up fee and/or substantial monthly service fees.
- The company demands a percentage of savings as payment.
- The company tells you to stop making payments to your creditors or communicating with them.
- The company requires you to make monthly payments to it, rather than to your creditors, but you're not participating in a legitimate debt management plan (DMP).
- The company claims that creditors never sue consumers for nonpayment of unsecured debt.
- The company promises that using its system will have no negative impact on your credit report.
- The company claims it can remove negative, but accurate information from your credit report.

You see many ads offering credit repair and fast and easy relief of debt. Many of these ads, however, are for scams. The FTC reports that some of the most common headlines to ignore include these: "Consolidate your bills into one monthly payment without borrowing," "STOP credit harassment, foreclosures, repossessions, tax levies, and garnishments," "Keep Your Property," "Wipe out your debts! Consolidate your bills! How? By using the protection and assistance provided by federal law. For once, let the law work for you!" Avoid services that use advertisements or sales literature with these or similar headlines.

Debt Consolidation

If you have multiple credit cards with balances and other types of high-interest loans, debt consolidation could help you. It involves taking out one lower-interest loan and using that money to pay off other loans and credit cards. Debt consolidation could save you a fortune in interest charges and help keep negative information off your credit report. Plus, you would pay just one monthly bill.

Debt consolidation is often used by people with multiple high-interest credit cards with high balances. However, it can also be used to help pay off student loans and other types of debt, because a debt consolidation loan will often be at a much lower interest rate than the debts it's consolidating.

There are several types of debt consolidation loans. Some people choose to refinance their mortgage and cash out some of their equity in the property in order to pay off credit cards or other loans. You could also apply for a home equity loan, a second mortgage, or another type of personal loan to consolidate your debts. Another option is to apply for a low-interest credit card and transfer your high-interest card balances to that new card.

If used properly, a debt consolidation loan can help you regain control over your debt, pay off past due accounts, and save a lot in interest fees. Contact your financial institution, mortgage broker, bank, or financial planner for information about how a debt consolidation loan could potentially help you deal with financial or credit problems. This is not a solution for everyone. Whether or not you could benefit from a debt consolidation loan will depend on your personal situation.

SMART-DEBT STRATEGY

Some companies that offer debt consolidation loans or mortgage refinancing for debt consolidation purposes charge hidden fees and other fees in the form of "points" and closing costs. Or, they charge high interest rates, especially to borrowers with below-average credit. Make sure you understand the loan you're being offered and the rates and fees and you deter-

---

mine that the loan will actually save you money after the consolidation process is complete. Understand exactly how the debt consolidation loan will benefit you in your specific situation. Simply trading several high-interest credit card debts for one new high-interest debt isn't beneficial unless it can improve your credit score, bring you up-to-date with your creditors, and enable you to pay off your debt. If that happens, in six months to one year, you'll qualify for a loan at a much lower interest rate and will have dramatically improved your credit situation.

Seek Out the Help You Need

If you find yourself in serious debt or experiencing major credit problems, whether because of circumstances beyond your control or poor money and credit management, don't be afraid to seek out help to fix your problems before they get too far out of control. There's no shame or need to be embarrassed about seeking out guidance from a certified, licensed, experienced, and reputable financial planner, accountant, or credit counselor. No matter how dire your situation, however, don't fall victim to a scam by believing a company's claims that your financial or credit problems can be solved quickly and easily, without actually paying off your debt. Find someone who is trustworthy and knowledgeable and who offers services you need and can afford.

Remember: even if you're in serious debt, there are organizations and credit counseling services that can help you, either for free or for a very small fee. Seeking out professional help with your financial problems could be one of the best investments you ever make, especially if you follow the advice that's offered and are able to eventually solve your financial and credit problems. There are very few situations that are so bad that they can't eventually be fixed, even if it means filing for bankruptcy and rebuilding your financial stability and credit rating from scratch. Filing for bankruptcy, however, should be considered only as an absolute last resort and only after you've consulted with a credit counselor or personal finance expert.

*   *   *

Now that you've acquired the knowledge you need to apply smart-debt strategies to managing your personal finances, loans, debts, and credit and you've hopefully developed a plan for fixing any negative financial problems you're currently facing, the final step is to create a plan for your future that will put the most useful smart-debt principles to work right from the start.

The final chapter of *Smart Debt* deals with making your money work for you through intelligent investments and planning for your future. Know your financial goals and develop a long-term strategy for achieving them through proper planning.

CHAPTER 10 | Improving Your Income and Planning for Your Financial Future

Thus far, from this book you've learned strategies for better managing, reducing, and eliminating your debt and for cutting your expenses. All of this has focused on getting the most out of the money you're earning currently. This chapter looks to the future and focuses on ways to earn a higher income, obtain a raise or promotion, or find a job that offers upward mobility and the prospect of higher pay.

There are many reasons why you'll want to focus on increasing your income over time, including the following:

- To be able to keep pace with inflation and rising prices without having to compromise your quality of life
- To pay off your debts faster
- To improve your quality of life
- To give yourself added financial security
- To achieve your long-term financial goals, such as buying a home or a car or putting your kids through college

Unless you discover that your current job is paying you considerably less than what you're worth in the current job market (for your training, education, experience, and skills in your geographic area and your industry), you should start implementing the strategies in this chapter immediately. However, it could take several months or longer before you start gaining the financial benefits.

It's important to understand that, if you work as an employee, your salary is based on your value to your employer. An employer's goal is to have you work as hard as possible and apply your skills and talents, yet pay you as little as possible in order to earn higher profits. How much you get paid is almost always a business decision based on the company's finances. It's typically not a personal decision.

The first step is to perceive yourself as an employer perceives you, to know what the employer values, and then work on improving upon whatever makes you valuable as an employee. No matter what the job or the industry, most employers value the following in their employees:

- education
- job-specific training
- skills
- experience
- personality, attitude, and dedication

By obtaining additional training, improving your education, gaining more work-related experience, and/or expanding your skills, you become more valuable to employers. Consider what you offer right now in each of these areas and then think about what you can do to improve and become more valuable to your current employer or future employers. What would it take to qualify for a promotion? How can you begin to better meet and exceed the employer's expectations in order to earn a raise? What new job responsibilities could you learn how to take on? What higher-paying positions in the company could you become qualified to fill?

Does your current employment situation offer upward mobility or are you stuck in a job that's going nowhere? A dead-end job won't lead to a raise or promotion or enable you to grow. A dead-end job might pay your bills right now, but it does not offer you the opportunity to improve your financial situation or quality of life. Since you want to be preparing for the future, if you're stuck in a dead-end job it might be wise to start exploring your options and seeking a better employment situation.

Ideally, you want to be working for a company that will evaluate your performance every six months, every year, or every two years and then be willing to offer you a raise or promotion based on that performance. At the same time, you want to find an employer that offers on-the-job training or that will encourage you to develop your skills and allow you to gain valuable experience through outside training. If an employer makes these opportunities available, it's your responsibility to take full advantage of them, even if it means investing extra time and effort into your job.

If your current employer doesn't offer training or encourage you to improve your skills, it becomes entirely your responsibility to find ways to do this yourself (on your own time), to improve your chances for better employment opportunities in the future. As you'll discover from this chapter, there are many ways to improve your education, obtain training, and expand your skills. But you must be committed to doing this and to investing your time and effort.

As you begin to explore ways to increase your income, whether with your current employer or elsewhere, it's important to do research to determine exactly what you're worth in the job market and then make sure you're being compensated fairly. Everyone wants a raise or a promotion, but are you actually worth more money for your education, training, experience, and skills than you're currently being paid? You'll learn how to determine this later in the chapter.

Finally, one of the most important keys to achieving long-term job or career success is to pinpoint what you're good at and what you love and then find a job with upward mobility potential that you're truly passionate about. You ideally want to follow a lifelong career path, not simply bounce from job to job with no upward mobility. When you follow a career path, each new job or position should come with better pay, increased benefits, and more opportunity to become a more valuable employee.

Finding a Job That's Right for You

No matter who you are, there are careers or professions in which you can succeed, based on your personality, your education, your unique interests, and your skills. Finding a job you're very good at doing is not good enough, however. Ideally, your job should also allow you to benefit from most if not all of your personal strengths. It should also involve performing tasks you enjoy.

Of course, in every job there will be things you don't like, but the trick is to make sure that the positives significantly outweigh the negatives. As you start your job search, look for a job you'll be passionate about. Otherwise, work will quickly become a grind or a drag that can make you miserable.

As you consider the types of work you'll enjoy, also consider what you want in terms of:

- The daily or weekly work schedule
- The salary and benefits you want and need
- The work environment
- The commute (distance, time, and costs)
- The type of coworkers
- The on-the-job responsibilities
- The on-the-job training for which you'd be eligible
- The career advancement opportunities

Look at the big picture so you can more easily identify the best job possibilities.

Defining Your Skills

Once you define the type of job you believe you'd most enjoy, the next step is to be creative and discover job possibilities that will require you to use your strengths and somehow involve your interests.

To help you define yourself and figure out what type of career you want to pursue, write down on a sheet of paper all of your marketable skills and abilities, as well as your interests, your hobbies, and the work-related activities that you really enjoy doing. Think about what work atmosphere would be ideal for you and what specific things you have liked and disliked about your previous work experiences. After you have compiled lists of your skills, likes, dislikes, and interests, think about where job possibilities might exist.

Your personal and professional skills can include any knowledge or ability that makes you more desirable and productive on the job. Depending on the industry or the type of position you want, your skills go beyond the core education you received in school. It includes any skills that will allow you to meet the responsibilities of your job, whether it's working the computerized cash register at a retail store or using specialized tools.

Being fluent in other languages, for example, can be an asset that will set you apart from other applicants for a wide range of positions. Other skills employers often want include sales, public speaking, management, leadership, typing, bookkeeping, filing, telemarketing, attention to details, and organizational abilities. Basic computer literacy is also important for many jobs.

When you find a job possibility, the "help wanted" ad or the job description provided by the employer should give you a good idea of the specific skills and training expected of applicants and what is particularly important. Determine exactly what the employer wants before you devise a plan for best promoting yourself, for conveying your professional and personal skills on the application form or in your resume and cover letter.

Simply stating you have a skill that's required for a job isn't enough. You'll want to mention every skill you have that's directly relevant to the job and then be able to provide specific examples of how you've used each skill in a work situation. In other words, you must prove that you possess each skill you list.

So, as you list each skill and describe how you've used it on the job, provide specific quantitative and qualitative details that convey the positive results of your skills. For example, if you list "ability to learn quickly," you might give as evidence "learned QuarkXPress on the job, helped graphic artists meet deadlines and keep customer worth $50K annually." You can provide written documentation or support materials later, during the interview.

Use your resume and employment applications to list all of your relevant skills and to briefly describe how you've used them. Then, in your cover letter, emphasize one or two of your most marketable skills or job qualifications so they stand out, without repeating information from your resume word for word.

Every marketable skill you possess has a value to an employer. Thus, having more relevant skills than an employer specifies will make you more desirable. You must show exactly how your particular combination of skills will make you a valuable asset to an employer.

By describing your skills carefully to according to the requirements of the job for which you're applying, you improve your chances of being invited for an interview. The interview is your opportunity to discuss your skills in person, provide details about your skills, describe how you've used them, and explain exactly how you could use them to meet the requirements of the job for which you're interviewing.

Your Previous Work Experience

For a potential employer, your work experience defines who you are and helps him or her decide whether you can meet the requirements of the job. It also helps a potential employer determine your value if he or she hires you.

Every employer, no matter the job, will want employees who offer more value than they cost. In other words, the question on a potential employer's mind will be "If I will be paying this person $X per hour, will he or she be worth that?"

In applying for a job, you must show your value to potential employers and show them exactly why they should hire you and what the benefits they will get if they hire you rather than another applicant.

As you apply for jobs, complete job applications, and participate in job interviews, make sure you can demonstrate to potential employers exactly why you're worth the salary you're expecting. They will be looking at your previous work experience for proof that you can meet or exceed the job requirements. If you can show how you've done that in the past, they will consider you more seriously.

Defining Your Interests

It's one thing to be good at your job. It's another thing entirely to enjoy doing it. As you seek opportunities, find jobs that involve tasks you enjoy and that best use your skills and interests. Try to find a job that you'll enjoy doing and that will challenge you. You'll be happier where your coworkers are friendly and the work environment is positive.

What interests you? What do you like? What do you dislike? Describe your dream job and then seek out a job that closely resembles that dream job or a job with career advancement opportunities that will lead you toward that dream job.

As you define your interests, likes, and dislikes, consider your work habits. Ask yourself questions like the following:

- Are you a "people person" who enjoys a lot of interaction or do you prefer to work alone?
- Are you independent, a self-starter, or do you work better with supervision?
- Are you satisfied with an hourly wage or a salary or would you prefer a compensation package that involves commissions, bonuses, and various benefits? What types of benefits are most important to you?

- Do you prefer a busy work environment or do you prefer a smaller, less crowded, quieter work environment?
- What are your weaknesses?
- What industry or type of company interests you?
- What tasks are you exceptionally good at?
- What tasks do you absolutely hate?
- What type of career advancement opportunities would you like in the near future and over the long term? Where would you like your career to be six months from now? What about one year or five years from now?
- What type of tasks would you prefer to be doing during your average work day?
- What type of work schedule would you like?
- What types of job responsibilities are you most skilled at handling?
- What skills do you lack that would help you get your dream job? How can you start building or expanding the necessary skills?

By answering these questions, you'll understand much better the types of jobs you should pursue. Knowing about yourself can help you avoid dead-end jobs that you'll hate. There's nothing worse than spending eight to ten hours per day in a job where you're miserable and that's leading you nowhere. The frustration, anxiety, and depression that can result will most definitely affect your personal life. While it's always important to focus on your financial situation, it's equally important to focus on your personal and professional wants and needs in order to achieve long-term success.

Always Look for Career Advancement Opportunities

Avoid dead-end jobs—they lead nowhere! There's no opportunity to advance, to earn more, to learn new skills. From day one on the job, you'll be doing the same thing, have the same responsibilities, and receive the same basic pay for the next one, three, five, or even ten years. For most people, this leads to extreme frustration.

There are many entry-level jobs that offer career advancement opportunities, but to pursue them, you'll probably need additional work experience, on-the-job training, new skills, and perhaps certification or a license. If you take an entry-level job with career advancement opportunities, from your first day start working toward your first promotion and pay raise by exceeding (not just meeting) your employer's expectations.

Make sure you understand your employer's expectations and the requirements for the job you're holding. Determine what it'll take to earn a promotion and/or pay raise. Then do what's necessary to obtain it, keeping it mind that it could take three months, six months, a year, or longer to achieve. Always be looking forward!

Every six months to one year, you should evaluate your status and your progress, determine what needs to happen to move your career forward, and decide whether you have a future with your current employer. It could be in your best interests professionally and/or financially to seek employment elsewhere, where your skills, experience, and qualifications will be better used and rewarded.

Make Sure You're Earning What You're Worth

Every employer, in every industry, strives to hire the most qualified, dedicated, and hard-working applicants possible for the lowest compensation possible. That makes it all the more important to understand what you're worth in the job market, as mentioned earlier.

Because salary information is often kept confidential at most companies, do research to ensure that your compensation package is totally fair and that your employer is not taking advantage of you.

Web sites like Salary.com (*www.salary.com*) and the Department of Labor (*www.dol.gov*) enable you to quickly research salary information for thousands of jobs in any geographic area. Many other career-related Web sites also profile popular industries and careers and provide related salary information.

As you try to determine if you're getting what you're worth in the job market, keep in mind there's a huge difference between your actual worth and your perceived value. People generally think they're overworked and underpaid. What are other people with similar qualifications, holding the same type of job in your geographic area, actually being paid? When you know the answer to this question, you'll more easily determine if you're being paid what you're worth.

It could make sense to accept a job that starts at a slightly lower salary if you're virtually guaranteed a raise or promotion within six months to one year, assuming you perform up to or beyond the expectations of the employer. Keep your eye on the big picture and think toward the future.

Remember: Benefits Are Worth Money Too

It's not all about your paycheck. Benefits all have a financial value, too. For example, if your employer provides health insurance, you don't need to pay for it. Even paid vacation time has a financial value. Know what benefits are being offered, determine what benefits are important to you, and then consider the value of those benefits as part of your overall compensation package.

It could definitely be worth it to accept a job for a slightly lower salary if there are valuable benefits that will reduce your expenses. Calculate the value of the entire compensation package before making any decisions.

Where to Find the Best Job Opportunities

There are many ways to learn about job openings. To find the best possibilities, try two or three of the methods described in this chapter. Don't rely on only the "help wanted" section of your local newspaper, for example, or only the online-based career-related Web sites.

CAREER-RELATED WEB SITES

Access to the Internet puts the most powerful job search tool at your disposal, 24/7. If you don't have access to the Internet from home, visit a library or an Internet café.

Many of the career-related Web sites offer extensive information about specific jobs, careers, and industries, as well as job listings. In addition to the general interest career-related Web sites listed in this section, consider visiting the Web sites operated by specific companies where you'd like to work (check under "Job Openings" or "Careers") and industry-oriented Web sites hosted by professional trade associations, for example.

For job listings and career-related information, the following Web sites are excellent resources:

- **CareerBuilder.com**—*www.careerbuilder.com*
- **Careers.org**—*www.careers.org*
- **Craigslist**—*www.craigslist.org* (choose the closest city listed, then the job listings)
- **EmploymentGuide.com**—*jobs.employmentguide.com/home*
- **Federal Job Search**—*www.federaljobsearch.com*
- **JobBank USA**—*www.jobbankusa.com*

- **Jobs.net**—*www.jobs.net*
- **Monster**—*www.monster.com*
- **USAJOBS**—*www.usajobs.opm.gov*
- **Yahoo! HotJobs**—*hotjobs.yahoo.com*
- **SummerJobs.com**—*www.summerjobs.com*

On these Web sites, you'll find job listings, informative articles, details about specific jobs and industries, and career-related advice. You'll also have the opportunity to post your resume online, so employers can find you.

JOB FAIRS

Job fairs are an excellent opportunity to meet potential employers in a relatively informal environment. You'll discover career fairs in virtually every city across America. Some focus on entry-level jobs while others are for specific industries. For example, TechExpoUSA (*www.techexpousa.com*) hosts fairs that focus on technical, computer-related jobs. Many high schools and colleges host job fairs. Others are advertised in local newspapers or on career-related Web sites.

When you attend a job fair, dress as if you're going to a formal job interview. Bring at least a dozen copies of your resume. There are often human resources professionals looking to hire people immediately. If you make a positive first impression, you could be hired on the spot or at least invited to interview.

NETWORKING

Networking is an extremely powerful job search tool. Many of the best openings are never advertised. You find out about them through networking with friends, family members, co-workers and former co-workers, your school's employment/career guidance office, or even your barber or hairstylist. Word-of-mouth and personalized introductions are great ways to find job opportunities, advertised or not. You can also network online, through services like MySpace (*www.myspace.com*), industry-oriented message boards, or even online chat rooms.

Let people know what type of job you're looking for and where you'd like to work. Ask people if they know anyone who can help make an introduction for you into a company. Seek out referrals and advice from the people you know. You may find that someone you know knows someone who knows of a job opening that's perfect for you.

Another way to network is to attend trade shows and industry-oriented conferences and introduce yourself to as many people as you can. Explain that you're looking for a job and the type of job and don't be afraid to ask for referrals or advice. Most employers are more apt to hire someone who comes highly recommended by a current employee, for example, than someone who simply walks in off the street after sending in a resume.

"HELP WANTED" ADS

Newspaper "help wanted" ads can often be an excellent resource for jobs in your geographic area. However, you must act immediately on any ad that interests you. If an ad in Sunday's newspaper catches your attention, respond to it the very first thing Monday morning. If you wait until later in the week, that employer will most likely have already received dozens of resumes, which puts you at a disadvantage.

Before you respond to an ad, make sure you're actually qualified for the job. Then, follow the directions in the ad carefully. If it says to fax or e-mail your resume, don't send it by mail. Don't try calling if the ad specifies, "No phone calls, please." If the ad requests additional information, besides your resume, provide exactly what's requested and in the specified format.

PROFESSIONAL TRADE ASSOCIATIONS AND UNIONS

Professional trade associations and unions are typically nonprofit organizations made up of employers and employees working in a specific industry. These organizations often offer job placement services and training opportunities and maintain a database of related job openings. They may post their job listings online, publish them in a trade magazine, or make them available to anyone who calls the organization. Trade associations and unions also hold meetings, seminars, trade shows, and conferences, which can be excellent opportunities to network.

CAREER GUIDANCE OFFICE AT SCHOOL

Most high schools, trade schools, vocational schools, colleges, universities, and distance-learning programs have a career guidance or job placement office. Here, you'll find information about job openings and resources to help you land a job. You might also receive help putting together your resume or preparing for a job interview. These services and resources are free of charge to current students (and often alumni), so be sure to take full advantage of them in your job search.

Reading industry-oriented magazines and trade journals gives you several advantages. You will learn about a specific industry that interests you and the latest trends in that industry. You'll also learn who the key players are and possibly which companies are hiring. Most industry magazines and trade journals publish job listings.

You'll find industry-oriented magazines and trade journals at large newsstands or libraries. Also, editions of these publications can often be found on the Web.

Improve Your Skills

If your employer offers on-the-job training, take advantage of it. If your employer will pay for outside education, be willing to invest the time and effort. No matter what types of skills or knowledge you need to get a better job, earn a raise, or obtain a promotion, chances are you can obtain that knowledge through one of the following methods:

- Attend night or weekend classes at a community college.
- Participate in distance learning or online courses.
- Participate in on-the-job training.
- Participate in seminars at industry-oriented trade shows or other events or in adult learning programs sponsored by local organizations, such as The Learning Annex (*www.learningannex.com*).
- Read books, magazines, and other industry-oriented publications.
- Return to school part-time to pursue a college or graduate degree or certification.
- Watch training videos and/or listen to books on tape.

The time and money and effort you invest now will be well compensated once you become qualified to get higher-paying jobs and take advantage of better career opportunities.

The Smart-Debt Principles Are a Way of Life

The smart-debt principles throughout this book can be applied to almost every aspect of your financial life. Learn them and act on them until they become second nature. Eventually, you should be able to apply these principles instinctively.

As you move forward, focus on doing the following:

- Pay off your current debt as quickly as possible.
- Control your spending so you're never forced to take on new debt. If you take on new debt, it should be your decision and you should do it properly, not out of desperation or absolute necessity.
- Find the best ways to make your money work for you, rather than wasting it on fees, finance charges, and high interest payments.
- Protect and manage—or, if necessary, rebuild—your credit rating and credit score, so when you want or need to use credit, financing, or a loan, you'll qualify for the best rates. An above-average credit score can save you thousands or tens of thousands of dollars on a mortgage, a car loan, or a home equity loan or on buying any big-ticket item.
- Develop, manage, and stick to a budget for yourself and your family.
- Eliminate all frivolous spending.
- Learn to use your credit cards wisely.
- Make sure that whenever you buy anything, the purchase is based on need. Then make intelligent decisions so you get the best price.

By always following these guidelines and the smart-debt strategies throughout this book, you'll be well on your way to long-term financial strength and stability. This stability will enable you to ultimately achieve your financial goals, improve your quality of life, and make the most of your money.

Remember: if you have trouble following these guidelines or achieving your objectives, seek out the professional help of a financial planner, an accountant, or a credit counselor. Even if this help costs you a few hundred dollars, the long-term savings will be in the thousands.

Your ultimate goal should be to live free from debt. However, this isn't always feasible. So, if you're going to live with debt, make sure it's smart debt and that you manage it well. This will enable you to reduce your stress, make better use of your money, and lead a happier and more productive life.

You can read lots of personal finance books, take courses on managing money, and even hire professionals to help you, but if you don't invest the time and energy in following the advice you receive, your financial problems will never go away. Managing your debt and finances is entirely up to you.

| Glossary

The following is a summary of important mortgage, credit, and finance terms used throughout this book. Understanding these terms will help you become smarter about debt.

Adjustable-rate mortgage (ARM)—A loan with an interest rate that can change during the life of the loan. If the interest rate goes down, so does the monthly payment (in most cases). If the interest rate goes up, so does the monthly payment. There are several types of ARMs. Some mortgages start off with a fixed interest rate and convert to an adjustable rate after a specified period. The amount the interest rate can change is often subject to a cap.

Affinity credit card—A traditional credit card (Visa or MasterCard) affiliated with an organization, branded to show that affiliation, and entitling cardholders to special discounts or deals from the organization. Most affinity credit cards have an annual fee and a slightly higher interest rate, but the incentives or perks can be worth the extra costs.

Amortization—The repayment of a loan, such as a mortgage, in which part of the payment is applied to the principal balance.

171

Glossary

Annual Credit Report Request Service/AnnualCreditReport.com—A centralized service operated by the three credit reporting agencies (credit bureaus) that processes all requests from consumers who wish to receive their free credit report from each agency.

Annual fee—For credit cards, a charge that the consumer may be required to pay every year for the privilege of having a credit card, ranging as high as $150 per year, more generally required if there are special benefits for using the card, such as airline miles or a cash-back bonus.

Annual percentage rate (APR)—The yearly cost of using money, including all fees and costs for acquiring a loan or using credit, expressed as a percentage. All lenders and creditors are obligated by law to disclose the APR.

Annual percentage yield—The rate at which the holder of a savings account in a bank, a credit union, or other financial institution earns interest.

Appraisal—An estimate of a property's fair market value calculated by a professional, licensed appraiser.

APR—See *Annual Percentage Rate.*

ATM—See *automated teller machine.*

Automated teller machine—A device that enables the owner of a checking account or savings account to deposit, withdraw, or transfer cash, using a personal identification number (PIN).

Average daily balance—The figure used by a credit card issuer to calculate interest charges, determined by adding daily balances for the month and then dividing that total by the number of days in the billing cycle. The average daily balance is multiplied by the monthly periodic rate, which is calculated by dividing the APR by 12.

Balance transfer—Movement of the amount owed on a credit card to another credit card.

Balance transfer rate—The annual percentage rate (APR) that a cardholder will pay on the amount of money moved to a credit card from another credit card.

Base price—The price of a vehicle, including all standard equipment and the factory warranty, but without any added options.

Broker associate—The person who works for the mortgage broker who is a borrower's primary contact throughout the application, approval, and closing process. Also known as a *mortgage consultant* or a *loan officer*, this person will often work on a commission basis, based on the mortgage products he or she sells.

Cardholders' agreement—The "fine print" associated with a credit card, consisting of the terms and conditions, the fees, and all other information a cardholder should know pertaining to the use of that card.

Cash advance—Money obtained by using a credit card in an ATM, for which the cardholder pays a fee that is either invariable or a percentage of the amount withdrawn.

Cash-out refinance—The process of refinancing and borrowing more money than is owed on a mortgage in order to obtain cash. Also known as *equity take-out.*

Certificate of deposit (CD)—A form of savings plan offered by many banks and other financial institutions that pays a higher interest rate than a savings account but requires a specified minimum deposit that must remain in the account for a specified length of time, ranging from six months to several years, or the account owner will be assessed a financial penalty.

Charge card—A card that requires full payment of the balance before the end of the billing period, with no line of credit and no interest charged.

Closing—The formal sale of a property and transfer from seller to buyer, when the buyer also formally acquires the mortgage and pays all closing costs and the seller provides the title for the property.

Closing costs—All fees, charges, and taxes the buyer will be required to pay at the closing, possibly including payment for points, taxes, title insurance, and financing costs.

Correspondent lender—A hybrid company that offers borrowers the benefits of working with a direct lender and the flexibility of working with a broker who represents many mortgage products, typically at more competitive rates than ordinary brokers. A correspondent lender makes approval decisions and initially funds the loan, but then, upon closing the loan, the correspondent lender sells the loan to another lender for servicing.

Credit—Financial trust, fundamentally expressed in terms of an amount of money that a lender or a creditor is willing to allow as debt. Using credit costs money—interest and fees.

Glossary

Credit card—A plastic card issued by a financial institution for a revolving credit account, authorizing the cardholder to purchase goods and services up to a specified credit limit and guaranteeing payment. The institution bills the cardholder monthly and charges interest on any amount of the balance that remains unpaid and carries into the next billing cycle.

Credit card transaction fee—Any of various amounts a credit card issuer charges a cardholder for making a cash advance, paying late, exceeding the credit limit, and other uses or abuses of the credit card account.

Credit counseling—A service that helps people who have difficulty paying for living beyond their means, by showing them how to manage their finances better and/or by negotiating with their creditors.

Credit rating—An educated estimate of a person's creditworthiness, a prediction of the likelihood that the person will pay a debt and the extent to which the lender is protected in the event of default.

Credit report—A credit file disclosure compiled by one of the credit reporting agencies—Equifax, Experian, or TransUnion—that contains personal and financial information about a person, including name, address, phone number, Social Security number, date of birth, past addresses, current and past employers, a listing of companies that have issued credit to that person (including credit cards, charge cards, car loans, mortgages, student loans, and home equity loans), and details about his or her credit history.

Credit reporting agency (aka credit bureau)—Any of the three national bureaus—Equifax, Experian, and TransUnion—that maintain credit histories on virtually all Americans with any credit history and supply creditors and lenders with timely and reliable financial reports as requested.

Credit score—A mathematical calculation of a person's creditworthiness, in which a credit reporting agency applies a complex formula to his or her current financial situation and credit history and generates a number between 300 and 850. The national average is about 678. To qualify for a mortgage typically requires a credit score of at least 620.

Debit card—A card that transfers payments directly from the cardholder's checking or savings account, an alternative to paying by check or with cash, but without using credit.

Debt—Money owed, often through using credit or obtaining loans.

Glossary

Debt consolidation—The use of a new loan to enable payment of debts that are overdue and/or on which the interest rates are significantly higher than the rate to be charged on the new loan.

Debt consolidation loan—A type of mortgage product that enables a person, by refinancing his or her mortgage, to obtain cash to pay off outstanding higher-interest debt. A debt consolidation loan can be part of a new mortgage or a separate loan using home equity as collateral.

Debt management plan (DMP)—A means by which a credit counseling service can help people in financial difficulty pay off their debts systematically, through monthly deposits to the credit counseling service, which then distributes the funds to their clients' creditors.

Debt negotiation service—An agency that helps people in financial difficulties make contact with their creditors and that negotiates on behalf of their clients to help them reach agreements with the creditors that will make it easier to pay off or to settle their debts, depending on the circumstances.

Dispute—Formal notification of a creditor and/or a credit-reporting agency by a consumer who suspects that there is erroneous information in his or her credit report and a request for an investigation of that information, which must take place, by law, within 30 days.

DMP—See *debt management plan.*

Equity—The percentage of the value of a home that the owner actually owns, as distinct from the percentage owed to the lender (through a mortgage, for example).

Fair Debt Collection Practices Act—Legislation passed by the U.S. Congress in 1996 to amend the Consumer Credit Protection Act to prohibit abusive practices by debt collectors, by outlining the legal rights of consumers, lenders, creditors, and collection agencies.

Federal Trade Commission—An independent agency of the United States government whose principal mission is to promote consumer protection and to eliminate and prevent anticompetitive business practices, notably through its Bureau of Consumer Protection.

Fixed-rate mortgage–A common type of mortgage product for which the interest rate and all monthly payments remain the same throughout the life of the loan, typically 15, 20, or 30 years.

Glossary

Float-down policy—The codified practice of a mortgage company to lower the interest rate on any mortgages for which the rate has been locked if interest rates drop after the lock-in.

FTC—See *Federal Trade Commission.*

Gift card—See *prepaid card.*

Good-faith estimate—An estimate of all closing fees, including prepaid and escrow items and lender charges, that the lender or mortgage broker must provide to the borrower within three days after he or she applies for a loan.

Grace period—Time during which a lender charges no interest on credit card purchases. A grace period is typically between 20 and 30 days. For someone with a zero balance who then uses the card to make purchases, the grace period is the time between the day of the purchases and the day on which finance charges will start being added to the new balance. If no grace period is offered, finance charges will accrue starting the moment a purchase is made. For someone with a balance, a grace period does not apply.

Home Equity Line of Credit (HELOC)—A type of second mortgage that provides the borrower with a firm commitment from the lender to make a specified amount of funds available for a specified period of time, using the equity in the borrower's home as collateral. During the term of the loan agreement, the borrower can borrow any amount of money up to the credit limit at any time and as often as he or she wants and pay back the outstanding balance over time. The interest rate is adjustable and the interest is calculated daily. A HELOC has an annual fee. This type of loan can be used as a financial safety net that a homeowner taps only when and if it's needed.

Home equity loan—A type of second mortgage that provides the borrower one lump sum of money that he or she must pay back over a specified period of time at a fixed interest rate, using his or her home as collateral. As with a fixed-rate mortgage, the monthly payment on a home equity loan remains constant. Interest rates for home equity loans are typically higher than for mortgages, but lower than for other types of loans, such as credit cards or car loans. The home equity loan has tax benefits, but they're more limited than with a mortgage: Typically, borrowers can deduct interest on home equity loans up to only $100,000. One of the big benefits to this type of loan is that the money can be used for almost anything.

Glossary

House credit card—A credit card issued by a retail store chain, a department store, a gas station, or any other company that caters to consumers; good for use only for the products and services sold by the issuing company.

HUD-1 Settlement Statement—A document prepared by the closing agent that details all of the information relating to the sale of the home, including price, amount of financing, loan fees, loan-related charges, real estate taxes due, and amounts to be paid by the seller and the buyer. All of the information on the HUD-1 should correspond to details in the *good faith estimate* and *truth-in-lending statement*. At the closing, both the seller and the buyer sign this document; the lender keeps the original.

Identity theft—The unauthorized use of personal identification information to commit fraud or other crimes, such as using another's credit card to make unauthorized purchases or using another's identity to take out loans or establish credit in that person's name.

Interest rate—A charge for using money from a lender or a creditor, generally expressed as a percentage of the amount of the debt.

Invoice price—What the manufacturer of a motor vehicle charges the dealership for the vehicle, although in practice the dealer typically pays less because of rebates, discounts, allowances, and other incentives.

Lender—The party that funds the mortgage and to whom the borrower owes the money—a bank, a credit union, a mortgage company, an investor, or even the U.S. government.

Letter of commitment—A document from the mortgage broker or lender stating that an applicant has been approved for a mortgage, the amount of the loan, and the terms.

Loan officer—The employee of the mortgage broker who is a borrower's primary contact throughout the application, approval, and closing process. Also known as a *mortgage consultant* or a *broker associate,* this person will often work on a commission basis, based on the mortgage products he or she sells.

Loan-to-value (LTV)—The ratio between the value of the property and the amount of the loan. For example, a 20-percent down payment means an LTV of 80 percent and a five-percent down payment means an LTV of 95 percent. Many types of mortgages have a specific LTV as a requirement for approval.

Glossary

Lock/lock-in—An agreement in which the lender guarantees a specified interest rate on a mortgage for a certain length of time at a certain cost. A rate lock is not a loan approval.

Minimum payment—The lowest amount of money that a credit card holder can pay to keep his or her account from going into default, typically about 2.0 percent to 2.5 percent of the outstanding balance.

MIP—See *mortgage insurance premium.*

Money market account—A special type of savings account that invests in low-risk, short-term securities and pays a higher interest rate than traditional savings or checking accounts. Typically a money market account allows the account holders to write checks in order to access his or her funds, requires the account holder to maintain a minimum balance, and limits the number of deposits or withdrawals that can be made each month.

Mortgage—A security instrument used in most states, similar to a deed of trust, that creates a lien on the property that is recorded in public records, involves two parties—the person borrowing (mortgagor) and the lender (mortgagee)—and gives the mortgagor full title to the property and gives the lender the right to sell the secured property if the mortgagor defaults (a sales process called foreclosure).

Mortgage banker—A company that makes home loans using its own money and then sells the mortgages to secondary mortgage lenders such as Fannie Mae or Freddie Mac or investors such as insurance companies.

Mortgage broker—An intermediary between a borrower and a lender. Most mortgage brokers represent multiple lenders and typically offer a broader range of mortgage products than a traditional bank. Mortgage brokers earn a fee for the services they provide. Over 80 percent of home buyers in the U.S. work through a mortgage broker.

Mortgage consultant—See *loan officer* or *broker associate.*

Mortgage insurance premium—Monthly charge that a mortgage holder pays for mortgage insurance, usually as part of the mortgage payment.

Mortgage preapproval—A commitment from a lender to an applicant for a mortgage, after an in-depth process, assuming that all of the borrower's qualifications remain intact at the time of the purchase and allowing for negation of the preapproval in case of a sudden increase in debt, drop in income, or drop in a credit score.

Glossary

Mortgage prequalification—An estimate of the size of the mortgage for which an applicant could qualify that a mortgage broker or lender can provides based on the applicant's credit history, credit score, debt, and income. The prequalification process is not binding and does not require the borrower to provide any formal financial documentation or complete a detailed application.

National Foundation for Credit Counseling (NFCC)—An organization whose mission is to set the national standard for quality credit counseling, debt reduction services, and education for financial wellness, through its member agencies.

Over-the-limit fee—Charge that a credit card holder pays if the total of his or her charges and fees exceed his or her credit limit within a billing cycle.

PMI—See *private mortgage insurance.*

Point—A fee that a borrower pays to the lender or broker, one percent of the loan amount.

Premium credit card—Credit card that offers incentives, such as cash-back rebates on purchases, frequent flier miles, insurance, etc. Premium credit cards offer high credit limits and are usually available only to people with excellent credit. An affinity card can also be a premium credit card.

Prepaid card—A card with the Visa or MasterCard logo that is accepted wherever major credit cards are accepted, but is not a credit card. It is basically a gift certificate: a person pays $X for a card and then can make $X in purchases. There's no need to open an account with a creditor and use of the card is not reported to the credit bureaus and does not impact the credit report or credit score. Also known as a *gift card.*

Prepayment penalty—A fee that a lender can charge the borrower for paying off the loan.

Prime rate—The interest rate at which commercial financial institutions make short-term loans to borrowers whose credit is so good that there is little risk to the lender. This rate fluctuates based on economic conditions and may differ among financial institutions. The prime rate serves as a basis for the interest rates charged for other loans for which the risk is higher.

Principal—The amount of money borrowed, not including interest, taxes, or insurance premiums associated with the mortgage.

Private mortgage insurance (PMI)—Policy typically required by lenders of borrowers applying for a conventional mortgage but unable to pay 20 percent down, which guarantees the lender will be paid even if the borrower defaults on the loan. The lower the down payment, the higher the cost of this insurance, which is added to the monthly payment. Once the borrower owns at least 20-percent equity in the home, this insurance can be canceled and the mortgage can be adjusted accordingly.

Purchase and sale agreement—A written and legally binding contract that both the buyer and the seller sign, outlining the terms, conditions, contingencies, and timetable for the sale of a property and describing the rights of the buyer and the seller pertaining to the transaction.

Refinance (aka refi)—The process by which a mortgagor pays off a loan with the proceeds from a new loan, typically using the same property as security for the new loan. The goal is typically to obtain a lower interest rate, reduce the monthly payment, shorten the duration of the loan, or cash out some of the equity.

Rescission period—Three full days after receiving all required disclosures and signing loan documents in which a borrower is allowed to cancel a refinance mortgage. Federal law allows this cancellation (rescission) period for certain loan transactions secured by the borrower's home, but not for loans made to purchase, construct, or acquire a primary residence or for transactions secured by a secondary residence or rental property.

Revolving credit—A line of credit for which the customer pays a fee and is then allowed to use any amount of the funds at any time and is required to repay at least a minimum amount every billing cycle and to pay an interest charge on the outstanding balance carried over into the next billing cycle.

Savings account—A bank account that pays the owner interest on the funds in the account.

Second mortgage—A loan a homeowner can obtain in addition to his or her primary mortgage. Just as with a primary mortgage, the home is used as collateral. This second mortgage is totally separate from the first mortgage, with its own rate and terms. The lender for the second mortgage is not entitled to any proceeds from the sale of the home until the lender on the first mortgage has been repaid. Because the risk of default is greater, rates for second mortgages tend to be higher than for first mortgages.

Glossary

Secured credit card—A card that works like any other major credit card (Visa or MasterCard), but draws upon a special account managed by the card issuer that consists of money deposited in advance by the cardholder, an account that secures all purchases up to the amount on deposit. Most credit cards are "buy now, pay later"; secured credit cards are "pay now, buy later." This card is much like a prepaid or gift card, but with fees and a big benefit—that the account is reported to the credit-reporting agencies as a regular credit card; it's a way for people with credit problems to begin rebuilding credit.

Smart debt—Debt that has the lowest possible rates and fees associated with it; debt that was acquired based on absolute need, not frivolous purchases or irresponsible spending; debt that allows the user to improve his or her quality of life, not simply cover everyday living expenses or pay for past expenditures; and debt that comes with a plan, created in advance, for paying it off in the shortest term possible.

Sticker price—The price of a motor vehicle that by law must be displayed on a label in the vehicle window, with a list of the vehicle's base price, the manufacturer's installed options (itemized), the manufacturer's transportation and delivery charge, and the manufacturer's suggested retail price as well as the fuel economy.

Sub-prime borrower—A person who doesn't meet the approval guidelines for a prime rate mortgage, due to a below-average credit score, a negative credit history, lack of employment information, the inability to provide various financial documents or verifiable income, or even a bankruptcy.

Sub-prime lender—A lender or mortgage broker specializing in working with sub-prime borrowers and offering a range of home financing options with less strict or nontraditional approval guidelines.

Trade line—Each of the items listed on a credit report.

Truth-in-lending statement (TIL)—A document provided by a lender to a mortgage applicant that details information about the mortgage, including the estimated monthly payment and all of the costs associated with the loan, including finance charges. If any of these figures change prior to the closing, the lender will revise the TIL and provide the update to the buyer at the closing.

|Index

| Index

Index

Index

Scholarships
  applying, 120-121
  sources, 120
Second mortgage
  benefits of, 74-75
  defined, 71
  as home equity line of credit
    (HELOC), 72, 76-78
  and loan consolidation, 154
Secured credit card, 98-99
Services, with checking account,
  138-139
Shopping.com Web site, 142
Shopzilla.com Web site, 142
66 Ways to Save Money campaign,
  144
Skills, job
  defining, 160-161
  methods for improving, 168
"Smart debt" principles
  applied to auto buying or leasing,
    81-83
  applied to credit card use, 99-101
  applied to everyday expenses,
    128-129
  vs. bad debt, 5-7
  defined, 5
  vs. good debt, 5
  and mortgages, 69-70
  and student loans, 117-126
  summarized, 169
  as way of life, 168-169
SmartMoney magazine, 148
Software, mortgage calculation, 48-
  49
Stafford loans, 122, 123
Stated income/stated-assets mortgages, 55
Stolen credit cards, 112-114
Student advice, 125-126
Student loans
  alternatives to, 119

Free Application for Federal
  Student Aid (FAFSA), 122-123
from federal government, 122
parent, 122, 124
Perkins, 122, 123-124
PLUS, 124
private, 122, 124-125
smart debt options, 118-119
Stafford, 122, 123
taking on new, 119-121
worksheet, 11, 118
SummerJobs.com Web site, 166

T
Transaction feeds, credit card, 103
Transunion
  contact information, 24
  dispute with, 32
  obtaining credit score from, 25
  three-in-one report from, 25
Types of mortgages
  15-, 20-, and 30-year fixed rate,
    50-51

U
USAJOBS Web site, 166

V
Vehix.com Web site, 82, 88, 142
Veteran's Affairs (VA) loans, 60

W
Web sites, mortgage calculation, 48
Why Rent? Own Your Dream Home!,
  68
Worksheets,
  budgeting, 130-132
  credit cards, 105-108
  financial, 8, 9, 11, 12, 13, 14, 16,
    17
Worth magazine, 148

Y
Yahoo! Autos, 88
Yahoo! HotJobs, 166